Set List.

Dancing in the dark.
That's Entertainment.
Hero
Wonderful tonight.

CW00339458

The Gig Book

No. 1 Hits

Published by
Wise Publications
14-15 Berners Street,
London W1T 3LJ, UK.

Exclusive Distributors:
Music Sales Limited
Distribution Centre,
Newmarket Road, Bury St Edmunds,
Suffolk IP33 3YB, UK.
Music Sales Pty Limited
20 Resolution Drive, Caringbah,
NSW 2229, Australia.

Order No. AM997480
ISBN 978-1-84938-090-4

Compiled by Nick Crispin.
Text by Graham Vickers.
Picture research by Jacqui Black.
All photographs courtesy of LFI,
except page 5, Lonnie Donegan (Getty Images).
Music engraved by Paul Ewers Music Design.
Edited by Tom Farncombe and Adrian Hopkins.
Design by Fresh Lemon.

www.musicsales.com

Printed in China

This book © Copyright 2009
Wise Publications, a division of
Music Sales Limited.

Unauthorised reproduction of any part
of this publication by any means including
photocopying is an infringement of copyright.

Wise Publications
part of The Music Sales Group
London/New York/Paris/Sydney/Copenhagen/Berlin/Tokyo/Madrid

The Gig Book No.1 Hits

Introduction

No. 1 Hits are, well...exactly that. Regardless of genre, musical merit or anything else, their indisputable claim to fame is that for at least one week they made it to the top of the charts — usually when large numbers of over-the-counter sales of singles were the measure of popularity.

Not that they were called singles when the dominant format was still the 10-inch 78 rpm disc (and despite the 1949 launch of the 7-inch 45 rpm vinyl format in the US, the 78 lingered well into the 1950s). The advent of rock 'n' roll tended to polarise consumers between formats: romantic ballads like 'Three Coins In The Fountain' and 'Unchained Melody' somehow seemed to belong to the old 78 culture while 'Great Balls Of Fire' and 'One Night' looked forward to the rocking new era of the 45. However, to begin with at least, for the youth market it rather depended on what kind of record player your parents had.

By the 1960s the discs were all small, the mix of pop genres was wide and one of the first of many novelty records made it to the No. 1 slot. Lonnie Donegan was at heart an old-time jazz entertainer who, approaching 30, almost accidentally became the voice of disaffected youth with his frantic skiffle versions of recycled American folk and blues numbers. However, his No. 1 'My Old Man's A Dustman' was squarely in the old music hall tradition where he sounded rather more at home. As the decade progressed that top chart position was subsequently occupied by everything from The Rolling Stones' bluesy 'Little Red Rooster' to Danny Williams' smooth 'Moon River' and Procol Harum's impenetrable 'Whiter Shade Of Pale'. David Bowie and The Byrds made it too, as did another less traditional novelty song, 'Lily The Pink' by Scaffold, a trio

of Liverpudlians one of whom was Paul McCartney's stepbrother.

The 1970s saw even more variety with 'Mamma Mia' enjoying its first flush of fame along with 'Imagine', 'Heart Of Glass' and 'Video Killed The Radio Star'. During the 1980s The Clash, Madonna and Spandau Ballet reflected a further widening of tastes, as indeed did contrasting No. 1s from the campy, extrovert Culture Club and the reliably gloomy Sinéad O'Connor. The CD finally took off, taking discs down to a petite 12 cm...or less in the case of some singles.

Thereafter the pattern was set. Achieving No. 1 might make you no more than a one-hit, one-week wonder (while much stronger-selling songs could lurk at lower chart positions for weeks or months) but it was your moment in the sun. In a new spin-off from the video age, a song featured in a hit movie could also take on a supercharged life of its own, especially if a Canadian singer got hold of it, as Bryan Adams and Céline Dion demonstrated in the respective cases of 'Robin Hood, Prince of Thieves' and 'Titanic'.

By the time downloads took over from physical discs, the kudos of having a No. 1 hit was well established: in order to grab everyone's attention and money at the same moment in time, your record might not have to have everything, but it certainly had to have a magical *something*. Here is a book packed with many that did.

The 1950s

An early fifties No. 1 hit came from Frankie Laine, the Italian-American singer who would later be associated with stirring Western theme tunes and dramatic ballads like 'Jezebel'. However 'I Believe', was a traditional up-and-down-the-scale quasi-religious song that celebrated the hand of God in every raindrop. Along with 'Three Coins In The Fountain' and 'Unchained Melody' it typified the kind of well-upholstered ballad that formed the staple chart-topper of the early 1950s. By 1957 a new generation of No. 1s was starting to come onto the scene. Buddy Holly, Elvis Presley and The Everly Brothers all brought a touch of modified country music (Texas, Tennessee and Kentucky flavours) to the hit parade's pole position. L.A. group The Platters, meanwhile, had a soaring version of a classic 1933 Jerome Kern song 'Smoke Gets In Your Eyes', a track which was neither rock 'n' roll nor traditional ballad but some sort of memorable bridge between the two.

The Gig Book

Elvis Presley

6

I Believe

Words & Music by Ervin Drake, Irvin Graham, Jimmy Shirl & Al Stillman

© Copyright 1952 & 1953 Hampshire House Publishing Corporation, USA.
TRO Essex Music Limited.
All Rights Reserved. International Copyright Secured.

Three Coins In The Fountain

Words by Sammy Cahn • Music by Jule Styne

© Copyright 1954 & 1967 EMI Catalogue Partnership/EMI Feist Catalog Incorporated/Sammy Cahn Music, USA.
EMI Music Publishing Limited (50%)/Onward Music Limited (50%).
All Rights Reserved. International Copyright Secured.

1. Three coins in the foun-tain, each one seek-ing hap-pi - ness,
2. Three hearts in the foun-tain, each heart long-ing for its home.

thrown by three hope-ful lov - ers, which one will the foun-tain bless. Rome.
There they lie in the foun-tain, some-where in the heart of

Which one will the foun-tain bless? Which one will the foun-tain bless?

Three coins in the foun - tain, through the rip-ples how they shine,

just one wish will be grant-ed, one heart will wear a va-len - tine, make it

mine! Make it mine! Make it mine!

I Can't Stop Loving You

Words & Music by Don Gibson

© Copyright 1958 Sony/ATV Music Publishing (UK) Limited.
All Rights Reserved. International Copyright Secured.

(I can't stop lov - ing you), I've made up my mind,
(I can't stop want - ing you), It's use-less to

say,___ to live in me - mo-ries___ of the lone - some
say,___ so I'll just live my life___ in dreams of yes-ter-

time. - day. Those hap - py hours

that we___ once knew, though___ long a-go___

they still___ make me blue.___ They___ say___ that

time heals a bro - ken heart,___

9

Unchained Melody

Words by Hy Zaret • Music by Alex North

© Copyright 1954 (Renewed 1982) Frank Music Corporation, USA.
MPL Communications Limited.
All Rights Reserved. International Copyright Secured.

Verse 2:
Lonely mountains gaze at the stars, at the stars
Waiting for the dawn of the day
All alone I gaze at the stars, at the stars
Dreaming of my love far away.

All Shook Up

Words & Music by Elvis Presley & Otis Blackwell

© Copyright 1957 Shalimar Music Corporation/Elvis Presley Music, USA.
Carlin Music Corporation.
All Rights Reserved. International Copyright Secured.

A - well - a, bless my soul,— what's wrong with me?— I'm
hands are sha-ky and my knees are weak, I

itch-ing like a man— on a fuz-zy tree,— my friends say I'm act-ing
can't seem to stand— on my own two feet.— Who do you thank when you

queer as a bug,— I'm in love! I'm all shook up!— Mm
have such luck?—

mm oh, oh, yeah,— yeah!— My

1.

2.

1. Please don't ask what's on my mind,— I'm a
(Verse 2 see block lyrics)

lit-tle mixed up but I'm feel-ing fine— when I'm near that girl that I love best, my

Verse 2:
My tongue gets tied when I try to speak
My insides shake like a leaf on a tree
There's only one cure for this body of mine
That's to have that girl that I love so fine!

Great Balls Of Fire

Words & Music by Otis Blackwell & Jack Hammer

© Copyright 1957 Hill And Range Songs Incorporated, USA.
Carlin Music Corporation.
All Rights Reserved. International Copyright Secured.

One Night

Words & Music by Dave Bartholomew, Pearl King & Anita Steiman

© Copyright 1957 Travis Music Incorporated/Unart Music Corporation/Elvis Presley Music/R&H Music Company, USA.
Sony/ATV Music Publishing (UK) Limited.
All Rights Reserved. International Copyright Secured.

Verse 2:
Just call my name and I'll be right by your side
I want your sweet helping hand
My love's too strong to hide.

That'll Be The Day

Words & Music by Buddy Holly, Norman Petty & Jerry Allison

© Copyright 1957 MPL Communications Incorporated, USA.
Peermusic (UK) Limited.
All Rights Reserved. International Copyright Secured.

Capo 1st fret

Well,___ that-'ll be the day, when you say good-bye, yes,___

that-'ll be the day, when you make me cry. Ah, you say you're gon-na leave, you

know it's a lie,___ 'cause that-'ll be the day___ when I die.__ 1. Well, you

give me all your lov-ing and your tur-tle-dov-ing, all___
2. When Cu-pid shot his dart,___ he shot it at your heart,

___ your hugs and kiss-es and your mon-ey too.__ Well,
___ so if we ev-er part and I leave___ you,___

20

All I Have To Do Is Dream

Words & Music by Boudleaux Bryant

© Copyright 1958 Sony/ATV Music Publishing (UK) Limited.
All Rights Reserved. International Copyright Secured.

♩ = 100

When   I   want you,   in   my arms, . when   I   want   you,
(Verse 2 see block lyrics)

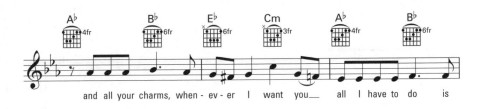

and all your charms, when - ev - er   I   want   you___   all   I   have to   do   is

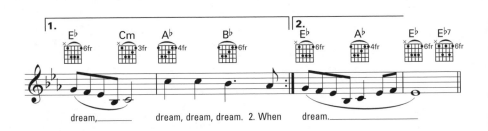

dream,_____   dream, dream, dream. 2. When   dream._____

I can make you mine,   taste your lips of wine,   an- y -time,   night or   day.

On - ly trou-ble is, gee whiz, I'm dream-ing my life___ a - way!___ I

need you so that I could die, I love you so

and that is why when - ev - er I want you___ all I have to do is

1.

dream._____

2.

dream._____

Dream, dream, dream,_ dream,_____ dream, dream, dream,_ dream.

Verse 2:
When I feel blue in the night
And I need you and all your charms
Whenever I want you all I have to do is
Dream, dream, dream, dream.

Smoke Gets In Your Eyes

Words by Otto Harbach • Music by Jerome Kern

© Copyright 1934 T.B. Harms & Company Incorporated, USA.
Universal Music Publishing Limited.
All rights in Germany administered by Universal Music Publ. GmbH.
All Rights Reserved. International Copyright Secured.

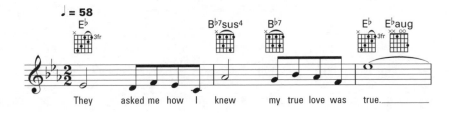

They asked me how I knew my true love was true.____

____ I of course re - plied, some-thing here in - side, can-not be de-

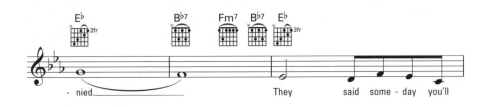

- nied.____ They said some - day you'll

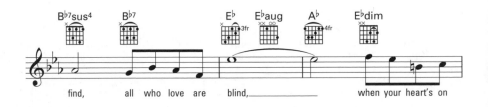

find, all who love are blind,_____ when your heart's on

fire, you must re - a - lize smoke gets in your eyes.____

So I chaffed__ them and I gay - ly laughed__ to think they could

doubt my love. Yet to - day_____ my love has

flown a - way,_____ I am with - out my

love. Now laugh - ing friends de - ride, tears I can - not

hide,_____ so I smile and say, "When a love - ly flame

dies, smoke gets in your eyes."_____

The Gig Book

The Kinks

The 1960s

Rock 'n' roll came of age in the 1960s with The Rolling Stones, Roy Orbison, The Beach Boys and of course The Beatles. If Tommy Roe's 'Dizzy' was a throwback to Buddy Holly, David Bowie's 'Space Oddity' showed the wacky way forward into the 1970s. The song's fortunes profited from the happy coincidence of the Apollo 11 moon landings for which broadcasters needed a suitably spacey theme, and the launch of the Stylophone, a futuristic-sounding electronic musical toy played by Bowie on the record. Nancy Sinatra, previously known only as one of daddy Frank's offspring, also had a No. 1 with the fetishy 'These Boots Are Made For Walking' produced and written by twangy guitarist Duane Eddy's old collaborator Lee Hazelwood. Ray Charles raided the country music songbook for a groundbreaking album from which his version of Don Gibson's 'I Can't Stop Loving You' went to the top of the singles charts, and, keeping the UK flag flying, came the breakthrough hit from that most British of groups, The Kinks—'You Really Got Me'.

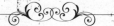

My Old Man's A Dustman

Words & Music by Lonnie Donegan, Peter Buchanan & Beverly Thorn

© Copyright 1960 Tyler Music Limited.
All Rights Reserved. International Copyright Secured.

folks give tips at Christ-mas, and some of them_ for-get, So when he picks their bins up, he
(Verses 3-5. see block lyric)

spills some on the step.   Now one old man got nast-y and to the coun-cil

wrote,   Next time my old man went round there he punched him up the throat.   Oh!

My old man's a   dust-man he wears a dust-man's hat,   he wears cor blim-ey trous-ers, and he

1-3.   **4.**

4° only (Vamp until ready)

lives in a coun-cil   flat.   (Next) *(Spoken interludes)*   time you see a   dust-man,

look-ing all   pale and   sad,   Don't   kick him in____   the

dust-bin, it   might   be   my   old   dad.____

1st spoken interlude:
I say, I say, Les
Yeah?
I found a police dog in my dustbin
Well how do you know it was a police dog?
He had a policeman with him!

Verse 3:
Though my old man's a dustman, he's got a heart of gold
He got married recently, though he's eighty-six years old
We said "Here, hang on Dad, you're getting past your prime!"
He said "Well, when you get to my age, it helps to pass the time!"

2nd spoken interlude:
I say, I say, I say
Yeah?
My dustbin's full of lillies
Well, throw them away then!
I can't, Lilly's wearing them!

Verse 4:
Now one day when in a hurry, he missed a lady's bin
He hadn't gone but a few yards when she chased after him
"What game do you think you're playing?", she cried right from the heart
"You've missed me, am I too late?", "No, jump up on the cart!"

3rd spoken interlude:
I say, I say, I say
What, you again?
My dustbin's absolutely full with toadstools
How do you know it's full?
Because there's not "mush-room" inside!

Verse 5:
He found a tiger's head one day, nailed to a piece of wood
The tiger looked quite miserable, but I suppose he should
Just then, from out a window, a voice began to wail,
He said, "Oi, where's me tiger's head?", "Four foot from his tail!"

Moon River

Words by Johnny Mercer • Music by Henry Mancini

© Copyright 1961 Famous Music LLC, USA.
Sony/ATV Harmony (UK) Limited.
All Rights Reserved. International Copyright Secured.

Oh, Pretty Woman

Words & Music by Roy Orbison & Bill Dees

© Copyright 1964 (renewed 1992) Acuff Rose Music Incorporated/Roy Orbison Music Company/Barbara Orbison Music Company, USA.
P & P Songs Limited (50%)/
Acuff-Rose Music Limited (50%).
All Rights Reserved. International Copyright Secured.

1. Pret-ty wo-man, walk-ing
(Verses 2 & 3 see block lyrics)

down the street._ Pret-ty wo-man, the kind I like to meet._ Pret-ty

wo-man, I don't be - lieve____ you, you're not the

truth, no-one could look as good as you.

Pret-ty wo-man stop a while,____ pret-ty wo-man
Pret-ty wo-man, yeah yeah yeah,____ pret-ty wo-man

talk a while,_____ pret-ty wo-man give your smile___ to
look my way,_____ pret-ty wo-man say you'll stay with

Is she

walk - ing back to me?_____

Yeah,_____ she's walk - ing back to me._____

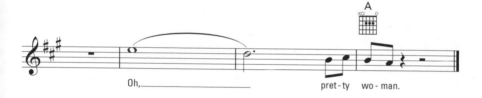

Oh,_____ pret-ty wo-man.

Verse 2:
Pretty woman, won't you pardon me
Pretty woman, I couldn't help but see
Pretty woman, that you look lovely as can be
Are you lonely just like me.

Verse 3:
Pretty woman, don't walk on by
Pretty woman, don't made me cry
Pretty woman, don't walk away
Hey, hey ok.

Little Red Rooster

Words & Music by Willie Dixon

© Copyright 1961 Hoochie Coochie Music/Arc Music Corporation, USA.
Bug Music Limited (70%)/
Jewel Music Publishing Company Limited (30%).
All Rights Reserved. International Copyright Secured.

1. I am the lit - tle red roost - er, too la - zy to crow for day.
(Verse 2 see block lyrics)

I am the lit - tle red roost - er,

too la - zy to crow for day.

Keep ev - 'ry-thing in the farm_ yard_

up - set_____ in ev - 'ry way.

3. If you see my lit - tle red roost - er,
please____ drive him home.__

If you see my lit - tle red roost - er,
please____ drive him home.__

Ain't had no peace in the farm____ yard,

since my lit - tle red roost - er's been gone.

Verse 2:
The dogs begin to bark and hounds begin to howl
Dogs begin to bark and hounds begin to howl
Watch out strange cat people
Little red rooster's on the prowl.

Glad All Over

Words & Music by Dave Clark & Mike Smith

© Copyright 1963 Ivy Music Limited.
All Rights Reserved. International Copyright Secured.

You say that you love me____ all of the time,

you say that you need me____ you'll al-ways be mine. I'm feel-in'

glad all ov - er,____ glad all ov - er. Ba-by I'm glad all ov -

- er so glad you're mine. I'll make you hap-py____ you'll nev-er be

blue, you'll have no sor - row____ for I'll al-ways be

true. And I'm feel - ing glad all ov - er,____

glad all ov - er, ba-by I'm glad all ov - er so glad you're mine.

Oth-er girls may try to take me a-way

but you know here by your side I will stay, I-I-I'll stay. Our love will last now___

till the end___ of time. Be-cause this love now_____

is on-ly yours and mine. And I'm feel-in' glad all ov - er,___

glad all ov - er, ba-by I'm glad all ov - er so glad you're

1. C F **2.** C F C

mine. So say that you mine._____

You'll Never Walk Alone

Words by Oscar Hammerstein II • Music by Richard Rodgers

© Copyright 1945 Richard Rodgers & The Estate of Oscar Hammerstein II.
Williamson Music Company owner of publication & allied rights for all countries of the Western Hemisphere & Japan.
Williamson Music Limited for all countries of the Eastern Hemisphere (except Japan).
All Rights Reserved. International Copyright Secured.

When you walk through a storm, hold your head up high and don't be a - fraid of the dark. At the end of the storm there's a gold - en sky and the sweet sil - ver song of a lark. Walk on through the wind, walk on, through the rain, though your dreams be tossed and blown.

Walk_ on, walk on_ with_ hope in your_ heart_ and you'll nev - er walk a - lone,_ you'll nev - er walk a - lone._ Walk_ ne - - - - ver walk a - - lone._

Mr. Tambourine Man

Words & Music by Bob Dylan

© Copyright 1964 (renewed 1992) Special Rider Music, USA.
All Rights Reserved. International Copyright Secured.

♩ = 122

Hey, Mis-ter Tam - bou-rine_ Man,_ play a song_ for me,_ I'm not sleep -

- y and_ there ain't no place I'm go-ing to._

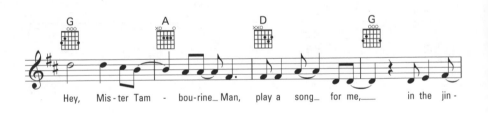

Hey, Mis - ter Tam - bou-rine_ Man, play a song_ for me,_ in the jin -

To Coda ⊕

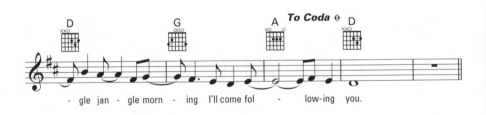

- gle jan - gle morn - ing I'll come fol - low-ing you.

1. Take me for a trip_ up - on your_ ma - gic swirl - ing
(2.) rea - dy to go_ a - ny - where, I'm_ rea - dy for to

ship, all my sen - ses have been stripped, and my hands
fade, un - til my own par - ade, cast your danc -

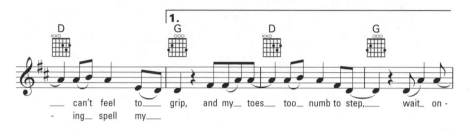

1.

can't feel to grip, and my toes too numb to step, wait on -
- ing spell my

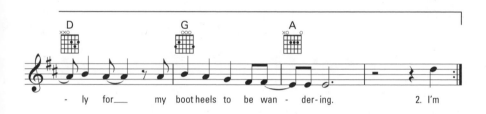

- ly for my boot heels to be wan - der- ing. 2. I'm

2.

D.C. al Coda

way, I pro-mise to go un - der it.

Coda

Repeat to fade

you.

41

You Really Got Me

Words & Music by Ray Davies

© Copyright 1964 Edward Kassner Music Company Limited.
All Rights Reserved. International Copyright Secured.

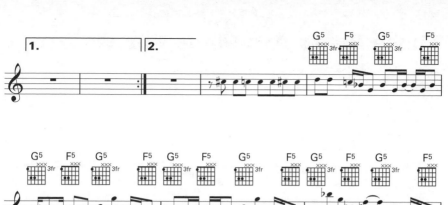

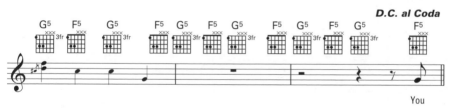

D.C. al Coda

You

⊕ **Coda**

D

Verses 2 & 3:
See, don't ever set me free
I always want to be your side
Girl, you really got me now
You got me so I can't sleep at night
Yeah, you really got me now
You got me so I don't know what I'm doing now
Oh yeah, you really got me now
You got me so I can't sleep at night
You really got me.

These Boots Are Made For Walking

Words & Music by Lee Hazlewood

© Copyright 1965 & 1966 Criterion Music Corporation(ASCAP)/Marada Music Limited.
Administered by Bug Music Limited.
All Rights Reserved. International Copyright Secured.

1. You keep say-in' you got some-thin' for me. Some-thin' you call love, but con-fess, you been a-mess-in' where you should-n't have been a-mess-in', and now some-one else is get-tin' all __ your best. These boots are made __ for walk-in' and that's just what they'll do. One of these days these boots are gon-na walk all ov-er you.

1, 2. 1° Yeah!

2. Are you read-y boots? Start walk-ing.

Verse 2:
You keep lyin' when you ought to be truthin'
And you keep losin' when you ought to not bet
You keep samin' when you ought to be a changin'
Now, what's right is right but you ain't been right yet.

Verse 3:
You keep playin' where you shouldn't be playin'
And you keep thinkin' that you'll never get burned
I just found me a brand new box of matches
And what he knows you ain't had time to learn.

44

Lily The Pink

Traditional
Arranged by John Gorman, Roger McGough & Mike McGear

© Copyright 1968 Noel Gay Music Company Limited.
All Rights Reserved. International Copyright Secured.

♩. = 121

We'll___ drink a drink a drink to Li - ly the pink the pink the

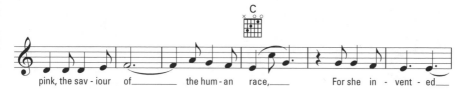

pink, the sav - iour of___ the hum - an race,___ For she in - vent - ed___

___ med - i - cin - al com - pound___ most ef - fi - ca - cious___ in ev - 'ry case.

1. Mis - ter Fre - ars___ had stick - y out ea - rs___ and it made him aw - ful
(Verses 3, 5, 7. see block lyrics)

shy,___ and so they gave him med - i - cin - al com - pound___ and now he's learn - ing___

To Codas I-III ⊕

___ how to fly. 2. Broth - er To - ny___ was not - ab - ly bo - ny,___ He would

45

C **G⁷**

nev - er eat his meals,___ And so they gave him med-i-cin-al com - pound___

C **G⁷**

D.S. al Coda I

___ now they move him___ round on wheels. We'll___

Coda I **C** **G⁷**

4. John - ny Ham - mer___ had a terr-ib-le st-st-st-st-st-st-stam-mer___ he could

C **G⁷**

hard - ly s - s - s-say a word,___ And so they gave him med-i-cin-al com - pound

G

(whispered) *D.S. al Coda II*

___ and now he's seen,___ But nev-er heard! We'll___

Coda II **C** **G⁷**

6. Jen-ni-fer Ecc - les___ had terr-i-ble freck - les___ and the

C

boys all call her names.___ But she changed with med-i-cin-al

com - pound_____ now he joins_____ in all their games.

We'll_____

D.S. al Coda III

Coda III
Rubato

8. Up to heav - en her soul_ asc - end - ed for the

church bells they did ring,_____ She took with her med - i - cin - al

D.S. al Fine

com - pound, Hark! The her - ald ang - els sing. We'll

Verse 3:
Old Ebenezer thought he was Julius Caesar
And so they put him in a home
Where they gave him medicinal compound
And now he's Emperor of Rome.

Verse 5:
Aunty Millie ran willy-nilly
When her legs they did recede
And so they hooked on medicinal compound
Now they call her Millipede.

Verse 7:
Lily the pink she, turned to drink she
Filled up with paraffin inside
And despite her medicinal compound
Sadly Picca-Lily died.

47

Good Vibrations

Words & Music by Brian Wilson & Mike Love

© Copyright 1966 Sea Of Tunes Publishing Company/Irving Music Corporation, USA.
Rondor Music (London) Limited.
All rights in Germany administered by Rondor Musikverlag GmbH.
All Rights Reserved. International Copyright Secured.

I'm pick-ing up good vi-bra-tions, she's giv-ing me ex - ci - ta - tions.

(Good, good, good, good___ vi - bra -

I'm pick - ing up good vi - bra - tions,

- tions.)___ she's giv - ing me ex - ci - ta - tions. Good, good,

I'm pick - ing up

D.C. al Coda
To Coda ⊕

good good___ vi - bra - tions.)_

good vi - bra - tions, she's giv - ing me ex - ci - ta - tions.

⊕ **Coda**

(Ah._____ Oh, my,___ my one e - la -

don't know where_ but she sends___ me there._____ Ah, my,___

- tion.)

Oh, my, my one e-la - tion.
my one sen-sa - tion. (My, my,

my one.)

Gotta keep those loving good vibrations a happening with her.

Ah.

Tempo Primo

(Good, good, good, good vi - bra -
I'm pick-ing up good vi - bra - tions,

50

- tions.___
she's giv - ing me ex - ci - ta - tions. (Good, good,

good, good_ vi - bra - tions.)

Na, na, na, na, na, na, na, na.

Na, na, na, na, na, na, na, na. Na, na, na, na, na, na, na, na.

Repeat to fade

Na, na, na, na, na, na, na, na.

Verse 2:
Close my eyes, she's somehow closer now
Softly smile, I know she must be kind
When I look in her eyes
She goes with me to the blossom world.

What A Wonderful World

Words & Music by George Weiss & Bob Thiele

© Copyright 1967 Range Road Music Incorporated/Quartet Music Incorporated/Abilene Music Incorporated, USA.
Carlin Music Corporation (50%)/
Memory Lane Music Limited (50%).
All Rights Reserved. International Copyright Secured.

peo-ple go-ing by.   I see friends sha-king hands_ say-ing

"How do you do?"   They're real-ly say-ing:__ "I love you." 3. I hear

ba - bies cry,   I watch them grow,   they'll learn much more

than I'll__ ev-er know. And   I think to my-self   what a won-der-ful world.__

— Yes,_____ I think to my-self,___ what a won-der-ful__

world.   (Strings)   Oh, yeah.

A Whiter Shade Of Pale

Words by Keith Reid • Music by Gary Brooker & Matthew Fisher

© Copyright 1967 Onward Music Limited.
All Rights Reserved. International Copyright Secured.

We skipped the light fan - dan - go_____ and turned cart-wheels 'cross the floor._____ I was feel - ing kind of sea - sick_____ but the crowd called out for_____ more. The room was hum-ming hard - er,_____ as the ceil - ing flew a - way.

54

Verse 2:
She said there is no reason
And the truth is plain to see
But I wandered through my playing cards
And would not let her be
One of sixteen vestal virgins
Who were leaving for the coast
And although my eyes were open
They might just as well been closed.

Dizzy

Words & Music by Tommy Roe & Freddy Weller

© Copyright 1969 Sony/ATV Music Publishing (UK) Limited.
All Rights Reserved. International Copyright Secured.

♩ = 103

Diz - zy, I'm so diz - zy my head is spin -

- ning, like a whirl - pool it nev - er ends.___ And it's

you girl mak-ing it spin,___ you're mak-ing me___ diz - zy.

1. First time that I saw you girl, I knew that I___ just had to make you mine.
(Verse 2 see block lyrics)

But it's so hard to talk___ to you with fel-las hang-ing round you all the

time. I want you for my___ sweet pet, but you keep play-ing hard to get, I'm

Verse 2:
I finally got to talk to you and I told you just exactly how I felt
Then I held you close to me and kissed you and my heart began to melt
Girl, you've got control on me, 'cause I'm so dizzy I can't see
I need to call a doctor for some help.

Space Oddity

Words & Music by David Bowie

© Copyright 1969 Onward Music Limited.
All Rights Reserved. International Copyright Secured.

♩ = 68

"Ground Con-trol___ to Ma - jor Tom,___

Ground Con-trol___ to Ma - jor Tom,___

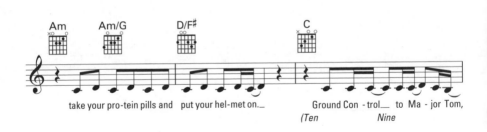

take your pro-tein pills and put your hel-met on.___ Ground Con-trol___ to Ma - jor Tom,
(Ten   Nine

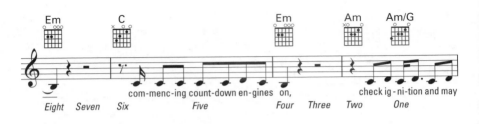

com-menc-ing count-down en-gines on,   check ig-ni-tion and may
Eight   Seven   Six   Five   Four   Three   Two   One

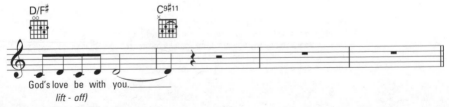

God's love be with you.___
     lift - off)

58

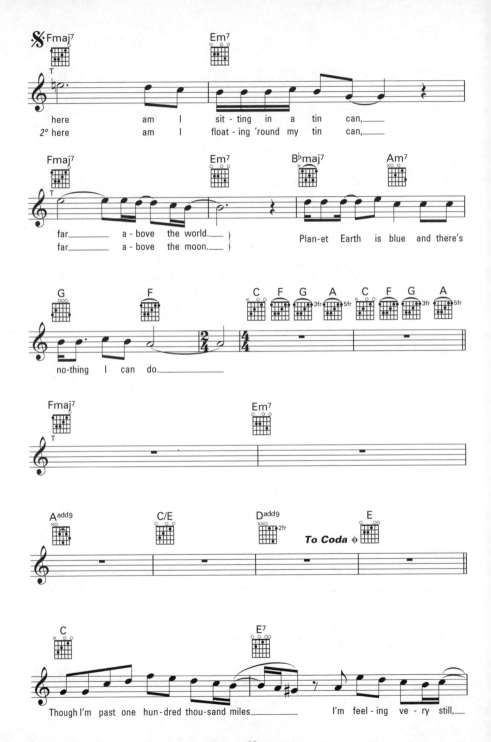

here   am   I   sit - ting   in   a   tin   can,___
2° here   am   I   float - ing 'round   my   tin   can,___

far___   a - bove   the world.__)
far___   a - bove   the moon.__)

Plan-et Earth is blue   and there's

no-thing   I   can   do.___

Though I'm past one hun-dred thou-sand miles___   I'm feel-ing ve-ry still,__

Something In The Air

Words & Music by John Keen

© Copyright 1969 Fabulous Music Limited.
All Rights Reserved. International Copyright Secured.

1. Call out the in-stig-at-ors, be-cause there's some-thing in the air.

We've got to get to-geth-er soon-er or lat-er, be-cause the

rev-o-lut-ion's here, and you know it's right.

And you know that it's right. We have got to get it to-geth-er,

we have got to get it to-geth-er now.

2. Lock up the streets and hous-es, be-cause there's

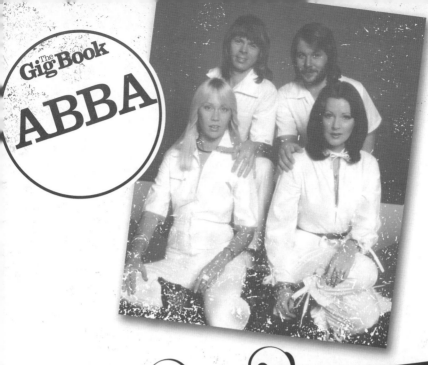

The Gig Book
ABBA

The 1970s

Generally getting a bad press for its music, the 1970s actually produced a bracing variety of chart-toppers even if its headline-grabber, punk rock, never quite made it to the No. 1 slot. John Lennon went all Utopian with 'Imagine' and George Harrison celebrated Hinduism with 'My Sweet Lord' while the hitherto rather fey T Rex suddenly started to boogie in earnest with 'Get It On'. Blondie's 'Heart Of Glass' was pure pop, albeit with a disco beat, and Slade introduced their durable Christmas crowd-pleaser 'Merry Xmas Everybody' to a grateful world. It was also the decade of 'Saturday Night Fever' and The Buggles as well as The Boomtown Rats and The Police. This was Abba's golden period too and also that of professional survivor Gloria Gaynor. But the seventies also had its sentimental side, witness Kenny Rogers' musical tale of agricultural infidelity 'Lucille', and Wings' maudlin 'Mull Of Kintyre', complete with bagpipes. The No. 1 with the most convoluted history was Roberta Flack's 'Killing Me Softly With His Song', a number written by Charles Fox and Norman Gimbel for vocalist Lori Lieberman who had herself already written a poem ('Killing Me Softly With His Blues') about her response to seeing Don McLean in concert.

My Sweet Lord

Words & Music by George Harrison

© Copyright 1970 Harrisongs Limited.
All Rights Reserved. International Copyright Secured.

♩ = 120

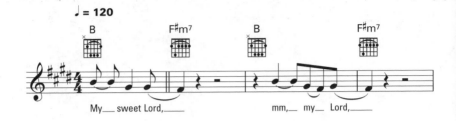

My___ sweet Lord,___ mm,___ my___ Lord,___

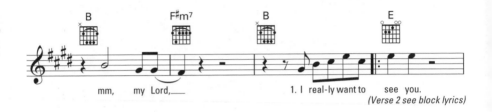

mm,___ my Lord,___ 1. I real-ly want to see you.

(Verse 2 see block lyrics)

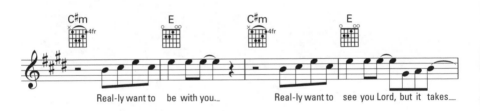

Real-ly want to be with you.___ Real-ly want to see you Lord, but it takes___

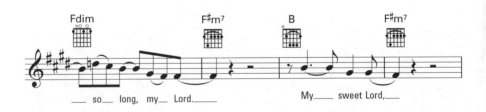

___ so___ long, my___ Lord.___ My___ sweet Lord,___

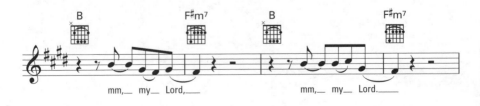

mm,___ my___ Lord,___ mm,___ my___ Lord.___

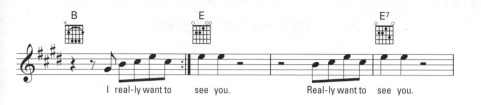

I real-ly want to see you. Real-ly want to see you.

Real-ly want to see_ you, Lord.___ Real-ly want to see you, Lord, but it takes_

___ so long_ my Lord,_____ my____ sweet Lord,_

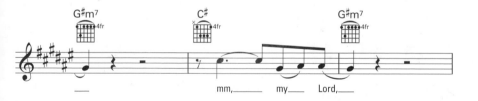

___ mm,_____ my____ Lord,___

my, my___ my Lord,___ my___ sweet Lord,

Verse 2:
I really want to know you
Really want to go with you
Really want to show you Lord
That it won't take so long, my Lord
My sweet Lord, mm, my Lord
My sweet Lord.

Maggie May

Words & Music by Rod Stewart & Martin Quittenton

© Copyright 1971 EMI Music Publishing (WP) Limited (50%)/
EMI Music Publishing Limited (37.5%)/
Warner/Chappell Music Limited (12.5%).
All Rights Reserved. International Copyright Secured.

1. Wake up Mag-gie, I think I've got some-thing to say to you.___ It's
(Verse 2 see block lyrics)

late Sep-tem-ber and I real-ly should be back___ at_school. I know I keep you a-mused___

___ but I feel I'm be-ing used.___ Oh, Mag-gie I could-n't have tried_ an-y

more.___ You led me a-way from home just to save you from be-ing a-

1, 2.

-lone. You stole my heart and that's___ what real-ly hurts.___ 2. The

3.

I sup-pose_ I could col-lect my books and get on back to school

68

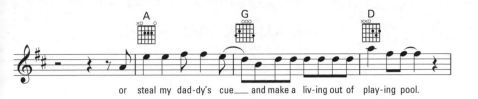

or steal my dad-dy's cue___ and make a liv-ing out of play-ing pool.

Or find my-self a rock 'n' roll band that needs a help - ing hand.___

___ Oh, Mag-gie I wish I'd nev-er seen your face._____

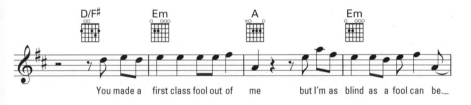

You made a first class fool out of me but I'm as blind as a fool can be.___

___ You stole my heart__ but I love you a - ny-way.___

Verse 2:
The morning sun, when it's in your face
Really shows your age
But that don't worry me none
In my eyes you're everything
I laugh at all of your jokes
My love you didn't need to coax.

Oh, Maggie I couldn't have tried any more
You led me away from home
Just to save you from being alone
You stole my soul
And that's a pain I can do without.

Verse 3:
All I needed was a friend to lend a guiding hand
But you turned into a lover
And mother what a lover
You wore me out
All you did was wreck my bed
And in the morning, kick me in the head.

Oh, Maggie I couldn't have tried any more
You led me away from home
Just to save you from being alone
You stole my heart
I couldn't leave you if I tried.

Imagine

Words & Music by John Lennon

© Copyright 1971 Lenono Music.
All Rights Reserved. International Copyright Secured.

1. I-mag-ine there's no heav - en, it's ea-sy if you try._____
2. I-mag-ine there's no coun - tries, it is-n't hard to do,_____

(Verse 3 see block lyrics)

No hell__ be-low__ us, a-bove us on-ly sky.__
No-thing to kill or die for, and no re-li-gion too.__

I-mag-ine all the peo - ple liv - ing for to-day.__ Ah.__
I-mag-ine all the peo - ple liv - ing life in peace,

You,__ you may say__ I'm a dream-er,

but I'm not the on-ly one.__ I hope some day__ you'll join__

__ us,__ and the world__ will be as one.__ live as one.__

D.C. al Fine   **Fine**

Verse 3:
Imagine no possessions, I wonder if you can
No need for greed or hunger, a brotherhood of man
Imagine all the people sharing all the world
You may say I'm a dreamer, but I'm not the only one
I hope some day you'll join us, and the world will live as one.

Killing Me Softly With His Song

Words by Norman Gimbel • Music by Charles Fox

© Copyright 1972 Fox-Gimbel Productions Incorporated, USA.
Onward Music Limited.
All Rights Reserved. International Copyright Secured.

Freely

1. Strum-ming my pain___ with his fin - gers,_____

sing - ing my life_____ with his words,_____

kill-ing me soft - ly with his___ song, kill-ing me soft - ly_____ with his__

___ song. Tell-ing my whole___ life___ with his___ words, kill-ing me soft -

- ly_____ with his song._____

a tempo ♩ = 119

2. I heard he sang___ a good song   I___ heard he

(Verses 3-4. see block lyrics)

had a style,___   and so I came___ to see him and

lis - ten for___ a while.___   And there___ he was___

___ this young___ boy   a stran - ger to my eyes.___

Strum - ming my pain___ with his fin - gers,___

sing - ing my life___ with his words___   kill - ing me soft - ly with his___

___ song, kill - ing me soft - ly___ with his___ song, tell - ing my whole___

life ___ with his ___ words, kill-ing me soft - ly ___

To Coda

1, 2. **3.**

___ with his song. ___ ___ He was

strum-ming there ___ yeah he was sing - ing my life, ___

D.S. al Coda

Coda

___ kill-ing me soft - ly with his ___ ___

Verse 2:
I felt all flushed with fever
Embarrassed by the crowd
I felt he found my letters
And read each one out loud
I prayed that he would finish
But he just kept right on.

Verse 3:
He sang as if he knew me
In all my dark despair
And then he looked right through me
As if I wasn't there
And he just kept on singing
Singing clear and strong.

Get It On

Words & Music by Marc Bolan

© Copyright 1971 Westminster Music Limited.
All Rights Reserved. International Copyright Secured.

♩ = 126

Well, you're dir - ty and sweet, clad in black, don't look back, and I love
- dy and wild, you got the blues in your shoes and your stock-

you. You're dir - ty and sweet, oh yeah. Well, you're slim
- ings. You're win - dy and wild, oh yeah. Well, you're built

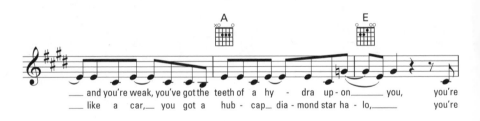

and you're weak, you've got the teeth of a hy - dra up - on you, you're
like a car, you got a hub - cap dia - mond star ha - lo, you're

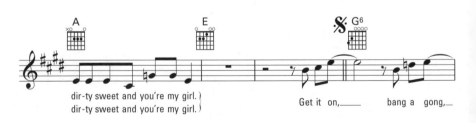

dir - ty sweet and you're my girl.
dir - ty sweet and you're my girl.
Get it on, bang a gong,

get it on. Get it on, bang a gong,

Merry Xmas Everybody

Words & Music by Neville Holder & James Lea

© Copyright 1973 Barn Publishing (Slade) Limited.
All Rights Reserved. International Copyright Secured.

1. Are you hang - ing up a stock - ing on your wall?

(Verses 2 & 3 see block lyrics)

It's the time that ev - 'ry San - ta has a ball. Does he ride

a red-nosed rein - deer? Does a 'ton - up' on his sleigh? Do the fair-

ies keep him so - ber for a day? So here it is: mer-ry Christ-

mas, ev - 'ry-bo - dy's hav-ing fun. Look to the fu-

ture now it's on - ly just be - gun. 2. Are you wait-

Verse 2:
Are you waiting for the family to arrive?
Are you sure you got the room to spare inside?
Does your granny always tell you, that the old songs are the best?
Then she's up and rock and rolling with the best!

Verse 3:
Are you hanging up a stocking on your wall?
Are you hoping that the snow will start to fall?
Do you ride on down the hillside in a buggy you have made?
When you land upon your head, then you bin slayed!

Mamma Mia

Words & Music by Benny Andersson, Stig Anderson & Björn Ulvaeus

© Copyright 1975 Union Songs AB, Sweden.
Bocu Music Limited for Great Britain and the Republic of Ireland.
All rights in Germany administered by Universal Music Publ. GmbH.
All Rights Reserved. International Copyright Secured.

1. I've been cheat-ed by you___ since I don't___ know when,___
(Verse 2 see block lyrics)

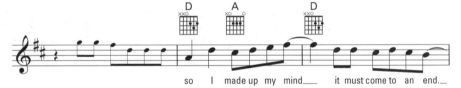

so I made up my mind___ it must come to an end.___

___ Look at me now,___

will I ev-er learn, I don't know how,___ but I sud-den-ly lose___

___ con-trol,___ there's a fi-re with-in___ my soul.___

Verse 2:
I've been angry and sad about things that you do
I can't count all the times that I've told you we're through
And when you go, when you slam the door
I think you know, that you won't be away too long
You know that I'm not that strong
Just a look and I can hear a bell ring
One more look and I forget everything.

If You Leave Me Now

Words & Music by Peter Cetera

© Copyright 1976 BMG Songs Incorporated/Big Elk Music, USA.
Fairwood Music Limited (10%)/
Universal Music Publishing MGB Limited (90%).
All Rights in Germany Administered by Musik Edition Discoton GmbH (A Division of Universal Music Publishing Group).
All Rights Reserved. International Copyright Secured.

If you leave me now__ you'll take a-way the big-gest part__ of me,

ooh,__ no,__ ba-by, please__ don't go.__

And if you leave me now, you'll take a-way the ve-ry heart__ of me,

ooh,__ no,__ ba-by, please__ don't go,__ ooh,

__ girl, I__ just want you to stay.__

A love__ like__ ours__ is love__ that's hard__ to find,

how could we let____ it slip____ a - way?____

We've come____ too far____ to leave____ it all____ be - hind,

_____ how could we end____ it all____ this way?

To Coda ⊕

_____ When to - mor - row comes_ and we both____ re - gret____ the

D.S. al Coda

things we said____ to - day.____

⊕ *Coda*

things we said____ to - day.____ If you

82

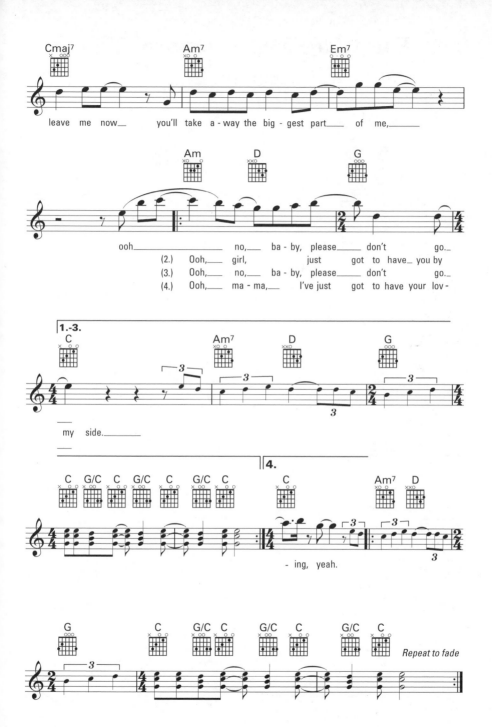

leave me now___ you'll take a-way the big-gest part___ of me,_____

ooh_____ no,___ ba-by, please_____ don't go.___
(2.) Ooh,___ girl, just got to have___ you by
(3.) Ooh,___ no,___ ba-by, please_____ don't go.___
(4.) Ooh,___ ma-ma,___ I've just got to have your lov-

1.-3.

my side._____

4.

- ing, yeah.

Repeat to fade

Knowing Me, Knowing You

Words & Music by Benny Andersson, Stig Anderson & Björn Ulvaeus

© Copyright 1976 Union Songs AB, Sweden.
Bocu Music Limited for Great Britain and the Republic of Ireland.
All rights in Germany administered by Universal Music Publ. GmbH.
All Rights Reserved. International Copyright Secured.

♩ = 105

1. No more_ care - free_ laugh - ter,_____
(Verse 2 see block lyrics)

si - lence ev - er__ af - ter._____ Walk -

- ing through an emp-ty house, tears in my eyes,__

this is where the sto-ry ends, this is good bye._____ Know-ing me, know-ing

you, there is no-thing we can do.___ Know-ing me, know-ing

you, we just have to face it this time__ we're through.

Verse 2:
Memories, good days, bad days
They'll be with me always
In these old familiar rooms
Children would play
Now there's only emptiness
Nothing to say.

85

Lucille

Words & Music by Roger Bowling & Hal Bynum

© Copyright 1976 ATV Music Corporation, USA.
Sony/ATV Music Publishing (UK) Limited.
All Rights Reserved. International Copyright Secured.

Verse 2:
In the mirror I saw him and I closely watched him
I thought how he looked out of place
He came to the woman who sat there beside me
He had a strange look on his face
The big hands were calloused, he looked like a mountain
For a minute I thought I was dead but he started shaking
His big heart was breaking
He turned to the woman and said…

Verse 3:
After he left us I ordered more whisky
I thought how she'd made him look small
From the lights of the bar room to the rented hotel room
We walked without talking at all
She was a beauty but when she came to me
She must have thought I'd lost my mind
I couldn't hold her, 'cause the words that he told her
Kept coming back time after time.

Mull Of Kintyre

Words & Music by Paul McCartney & Denny Laine

© Copyright 1977 MPL Communications Limited.
All Rights Reserved. International Copyright Secured.

Mull_ of Kin - tyre, oh mist roll - ing in from_ the sea, my de-

-sire is al-ways to be here Oh Mull_ of Kin - tyre.

Far have_ I tra - velled and much have I seen, dark dis - tant

moun - tains_ with val - leys_ of green. Past paint - ed des - erts,_ the

sun-set's on fire,_ as he car - ries me home_ to the Mull_ of Kin-

- tyre.

Sweep through the hea-ther_ like deer in the glen. Car-ry me back to the

days I knew then, nights when we sang like a hea-ven-ly

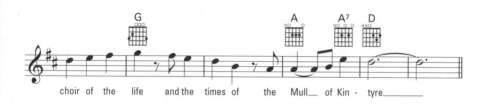

choir of the life and the times of the Mull_ of Kin-tyre.____

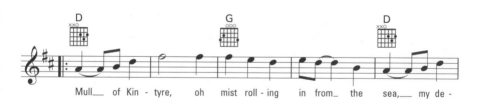

Mull_ of Kin-tyre, oh mist roll-ing in from_ the sea,_ my de-

-sire is al-ways to be there_ oh Mull_ of Kin-tyre.____

Repeat to fade

89

Night Fever

Words & Music by Barry Gibb, Maurice Gibb & Robin Gibb

© Copyright 1977 Gibb Brothers Music (66.66%)/
Crompton Songs/Warner/Chappell Music Limited (33.34%).
All Rights Reserved. International Copyright Secured.

♩ = 110

Lis - ten to___ the ground, there is move-ment all___ a - round, there is
(D.C.) heat of our___ love, don't need no help for us to make it. Gim - me

some - thing go — ing down and I can feel it. On the
just e - nough to take___ us to the morn - ing. I got

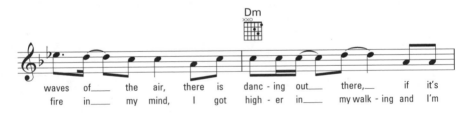

waves of___ the air, there is danc - ing out___ there,___ if it's
fire in___ my mind, I got high - er in___ my walk - ing and I'm

some - thing we can share, we can steal it.) And that
glow - ing in the dark, I give you warn - ing.) And that

sweet ci - ty wo - man, she moves through the light,___ con -

I Will Survive

Words & Music by Dino Fekaris & Freddie Perren

© Copyright 1978 Perren-Vibes Music Company/PolyGram International Publishing Incorporated, USA.
Universal Music Publishing Limited.
All rights in Germany administered by Universal Music Publ. GmbH.
All Rights Reserved. International Copyright Secured.

At

first I was a-fraid, I was pet-ri-fied,____ kept think-ing I could ne-ver live__ with-out you

by my side, but then I spent so ma-ny nights think-ing how you did me wrong and I grew

strong and I learned how to get a-long.__ 1. And so you're back from out-er space__
(Verse 3 see block lyrics)

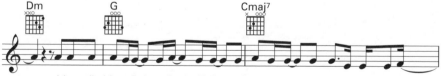

____ I just walked in to find_ you here_ with that_ sad look up-on__ your face. I should have changed__

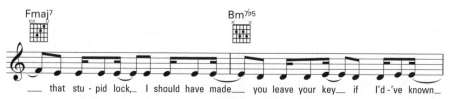

____ that stu-pid lock,__ I should have made__ you leave your key__ if I'd-'ve known__

93

Verse 3:
And you see me somebody new
I'm not that chained up little person
Still in love with you
And so you feel like dropping in
And just expect me to be free
Well, now I'm saving all my loving
For someone who's loving me.

You're The One That I Want

Words & Music by John Farrar

© Copyright 1978 Ensign Music Corporation/Famous Music Corporation, USA.
All Rights Reserved. International Copyright Secured.

You bet-ter shape up,___ you bet-ter un - der - stand

to my heart___ I must be true.___ Noth-ing left, noth-ing

left for me to do.___ *Chorus* You're the one that I want. (You are the one I want.)

1, 2. **3.**

You ooh, ooh, hon - ey. The ooh, are what I need.___

D.S.
D.S.S.
(Repeat Chorus to fade)

___ Oh yes in - deed. 2. If you're

Verse 2:
If you're filled with affection
You're too shy to convey
Meditate in my direction
Feel your way
I better shape up
'Cause you need a man
Who can keep me satisfied
I better shape up if I'm gonna prove
That my faith is justified
Are you sure?
Yes, I'm sure down deep inside.

Heart Of Glass

Words & Music by Deborah Harry & Chris Stein

© Copyright 1978 Rare Blue Music Incorporated/Monster Island Music Incorporated, USA.
Chrysalis Music Limited.
All Rights Reserved. International Copyright Secured.

1. Once I had a love___ and it___ was a gas___
(Verse 4 see block lyrics)

soon turned out   had a heart of   glass.___   Seemed like the real thing   on - ly to

find___   mu-cho mis-trust, love's gone be - hind.___

2. Once I had a love___ and it___ was di - vine,___   soon found out   I was los-ing my
(Verse 3 see block lyrics)

mind.   Seemed like the real thing   but I___ was so   blind,___

mu - cho mis -trust,   love's gone be - hind.___

98

In be - tween_ what I find_ is pleas-ing and I'm feel - ing fine,_

love is so_ con-fus- ing, there's no peace of mind, if I fear I'm los-ing you, it's

1.

just no good, you teas-ing like_ you do._

2.

La la la_ la la la la la la_ la la la la la la,_ la

la la la la la___ la la la la la la,___ la

la la la la la,___ yeah,___ rid - ing high on love's_ true_ blu-ish light._

D.C. al Coda

Ooh_ oh,___ ooh_ oh,___ ooh_ oh,___ ooh_ oh._

Coda E

___ Ooh___ oh,___

Repeat to fade

ooh___ oh.___

Verse 3:
Once I had a love and it was a gas
Soon turned out had a heart of glass
Seemed like the real thing but only to find
Mucho mistrust, love's gone behind.

Lost in time, adorable illusion and I cannot hide
I'm the one you're using
Please don't push me aside
We could have made it cruising, yeah.

Verse 4:
Once I had a love and it was a gas
Soon turned out to be a pain in the ass
Seemed like the real thing only to find
Mucho mistrust, love's gone behind.

I Don't Like Mondays

Words & Music by Bob Geldof

© Copyright 1979 Promostraat B.V., Holland.
Sherlock Holmes Music Limited.
All Rights Reserved. International Copyright Secured.

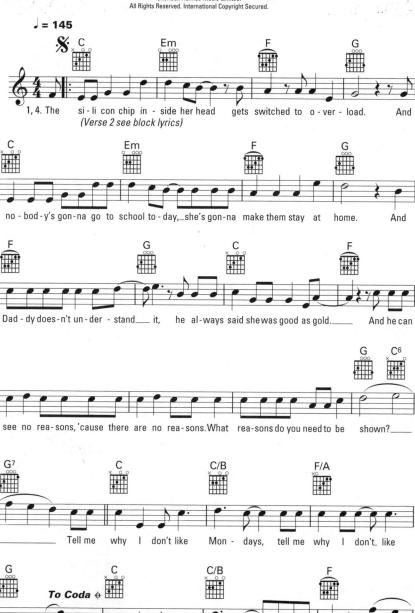

1, 4. The si-li-con chip in-side her head gets switched to o-ver-load. And
(Verse 2 see block lyrics)

no-bod-y's gon-na go to school to-day, she's gon-na make them stay at home. And

Dad-dy does-n't un-der-stand it, he al-ways said she was good as gold. And he can

see no rea-sons, 'cause there are no rea-sons. What rea-sons do you need to be shown?

Tell me why I don't like Mon-days, tell me why I don't like

Mon-days, tell me why I don't like Mon-days, I want to shoot, ooh,

To Coda

101

the whole day_ down.   2.The

the whole_ day down, down,   down, shoot it all down.__

2

3. And all the   play - ing's stopped in the

play - ground, now   she wants ⋅ to   play   with her   toys a - while.   And

school's out   ear - ly and   soon we'll be learn - ing and the   les - son to - day__   is

how to die.   And then the   bull - horn crack - les, and the   cap - tain tack - les with the

prob - lems and the hows and whys.__   And he can see   no   rea - sons, 'cause there

D.S. al Coda

are   no rea - sons. What   rea - sons do you need to__ die,   die?   Oh,_____ and the

why I don't like, I don't like, I don't like, Mon - days, tell me

why I don't like, I don't like, I don't like, Mon - days, tell me

why I don't like Mon - days;__ I want to shoot, oo,_____

the whole day__

down.

Verse 2:
The telex machine is kept so clean and it types to a waiting world
And mother feels so shocked, father's world is rocked
And their thoughts turn to their own little girl
Sweet sixteen, ain't that peachy keen
Now it ain't so neat to admit defeat
They can see no reasons, 'cause there are no reasons.
What reasons do you need?

Message In A Bottle

Words & Music by Sting

© Copyright 1979 Steerpike Limited/Steerpike (Overseas) Limited/EMI Music Publishing Limited.
All Rights Reserved. International Copyright Secured.

104

Verse 2:

A year has passed since I wrote my note
But I should have known this right from the start
Only hope can keep me together
Love can mend your life but love can break your heart.

Verse 3:

Walked out this morning, I don't believe what I saw
A hundred billion bottles washed up on the shore
Seems like I'm not alone in being alone
A hundred billion castaways looking for a home.

105

Video Killed The Radio Star

Words & Music by Geoffrey Downes, Trevor Horn & Bruce Woolley

© Copyright 1979 Carlin Music Corporation (50%)/
Universal/Island Music Limited (50%) (administered in Germany by Universal Music Publ. GmbH).
All Rights Reserved. International Copyright Secured.

I heard you on the wire-less back in fif-ty-two, ly-ing a-wake in-tent-ly tun-ing in on you. If I was young it did-n't stop____ you com-ing through.

Oh,____ oh.____

1. They took the cre-dit for your
(Verse 2 see block lyrics)

se-cond sym-pho-ny, re-writ-ten by ma-chine on new tech-no-lo-gy. And now I un-der-stand the prob-lems you can see. Oh,____ oh.____

I met your child-ren.__ Oh,____ oh.__ What did you tell them?

106

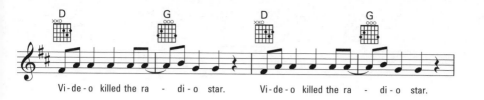

Vi-de-o killed the ra - di-o star. Vi-de-o killed the ra - di-o star.

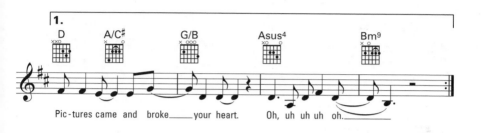

1.

Pic-tures came and broke___ your heart. Oh, uh uh uh oh.___

2.

In my mind_ and in my car,_ we can't re-wind, we've gone too far._

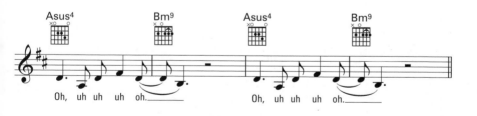

Oh, uh uh uh uh oh.___ Oh, uh uh uh uh oh.___

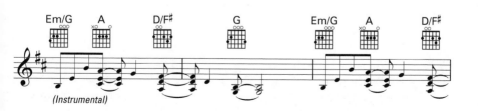

(Instrumental)

107

Verse 2
And now we meet in an abandoned studio
We hear the playback and it seems so long ago
And you remember how the jingles used to go
Oh, oh. You were the first one
Oh, oh. You were the last one.

The Gig Book
The Specials

The 1980s

Abba, Blondie and Bowie were still on a roll at the start of the 1980s, but soon the sounds of The Clash and The Specials showed there was still a bit of life left in the survivors of the 70s punk movement. Dexys Midnight Runners, Culture Club and Spandau Ballet were the signature bands of the period, but, as usual, some unexpected No. 1s went against the grain

of the times. Chicano rockers Los Lobos had arrived with a fêted album called *Will The Wolf Survive* before supplying the Latin-flavoured music for a film about 50s Hispanic rocker Ritchie Valens. Valens had originally put his rock version of the public domain song 'La Bamba' on the 'B' side of his hit 'Donna', but it became just as famous and subsequently gave its name to the Valens biopic. Los Lobos' version of 'La Bamba' made No. 1. Frankie Goes To Hollywood scored with one of several different songs all called 'The Power Of Love' and Madonna slipped in under the wire at the end of the decade with the first single pulled from her fourth album 'Like A Prayer'.

Going Underground

Words & Music by Paul Weller

© Copyright 1980 Stylist Music Limited.
Universal Music Publishing MGB Limited.
All Rights in Germany Administered by Musik Edition Discoton GmbH (A Division of Universal Music Publishing Group).
All Rights Reserved. International Copyright Secured.

1. Some peo - ple might say my life is in a rut. I'm quite
(Verse 2 see block lyrics)

hap - py with what I got. Peo - ple might say that I should strive for

more, but I'm so hap - py I can't see the point. Some - thing's hap - pen - ing

here to - day__ a show of strength__ with your boys bri - gade__ and

I'm so hap - py and you're__ so kind,__ you want more mo - ney, of course__

__ I don't mind__ to buy nu - cle - ar text__ books for at - om - ic crimes__ and the

112

pub - lic gets___ what the pub - lic wants,___ but I want no-thing this so -

- ci - e - ty's got___'cause I'm go-ing un - der-ground, (go-ing un - der-ground) well let the

brass bands play and feet start to pound.___ Go - ing un - der - ground,___ (go - ing

un - der - ground) well let the boys all sing and let the boys all shout for to -

2° so

1.

2.

-mor-row.   - mor - row._____ la,___ la, la, la,
(Ho)

(Ho) la,___ la la la. We talk and we talk un-til my head ex - plodes. I

turn on the news and my bo - dy froze.___ Bray-ing sheep on my

113

Verse 2:
Some people might get some pleasure out of hate
Me, I've enough already on my plate
People might need some tension to relax
I'm too busy dodging 'tween the flak
When you see here's a what you get
You made your bed you better lie in it
You choose your leaders and place your trust
As their lies wash you down and their promises rust
You'll see kidney machines are replaced by rockets and guns
And the public wants what the public gets
But I don't care what this society wants.

The Tide Is High

Words & Music by John Holt, Howard Barrett & Tyrone Evans

© Copyright 1968 & 1972 The Sparta Florida Music Group Limited
All Rights Reserved. International Copyright Secured.

♩ = 88

The tide is high but I'm hold-ing on, I'm gon-na be your num-ber one.

I'm___ not the kind-a girl who gives up just___ like that,___ oh,

no.___ It's not the things you do that tease and hurt me bad,

but it's the way you do the things you do to me. I'm___ not the kind-a girl

who gives up just___ like that,___ oh, no.___ The

tide is high but I'm hold-ing on, I'm gon-na be your num-ber one,

116

num - ber one.____ Ev-'ry girl wants you to be her man,

but I'll wait, my dear, till it's my____ turn. I'm___ not the kind - a girl

who gives up just_ like that,_ oh, no.____ The tide is high but I'm

hold - ing on, I'm gon-na be your num - ber one, num - ber one,

num - ber one.____

D.S. al Coda

To Coda ⊕

⊕ Coda

Repeat to fade

__ The tide is high but I'm hold - ing on, I'm gon - na be your num - ber one. The

117

Ashes To Ashes

Words & Music by David Bowie

© Copyright 1980 Tintoretto Music/RZO Music Limited (84%)/
EMI Music Publishing Limited (16%).
All Rights Reserved. International Copyright Secured.

♩ = 120
Capo 1st fret

1. Do you re - mem-ber a guy___ that's been___ in such an
(Verse 2 see block lyrics)

ear - ly song?_____ I've heard a ru-mour from Ground___ Con - trol,___

oh no,___ don't say it's true.___ They got a mes-sage from the

Ac - tion Man. I'm hap - py, hope you're hap - py too.___

I've loved all___ I've___ need-ed love,___ sor - did___ de -

-tails fol - low - ing: The shriek-ing of no-thing is kill - ing just,

118

Verse 2:
Time and again I tell myself
I'll stay clean tonight
But the little green wheels are following me
Oh no, not again
I'm stuck with a valuable friend
I'm happy, hope you're happy too
One flash of light but no smoking pistol
I've never done good things
I've never done bad things
I never did anything out of the blue
Want an axe to break the ice
Want to come down right now.

The Winner Takes It All

Words & Music by Benny Andersson & Björn Ulvaeus

© Copyright 1980 Union Songs AB, Sweden.
Bocu Music Limited for Great Britain and the Republic of Ireland.
All rights in Germany administered by Universal Music Publ. GmbH.
All Rights Reserved. International Copyright Secured.

(Verses 2-4. see block lyrics)

1. I don't wan-na talk a-bout things we've gone through, though it's hurt-ing me, now___ it's his-to-ry. I played all my cards and that's what you've done too, noth-ing more to say, no more ace to play. The win-ner takes it

all,   the los - er stand - ing small

be - side the vic - to - ry,_____ that's___ her des - ti-

1. - ny._____ 2. I was in your ___ **2, 3.** The win - ner takes it

all,   the los - er has to fall,

it's sim - ple and it's plain,_____

why____ should I com - plain_____

1. ___ 3. But tell me, does she _____ **2.** *D.S. al Coda* 4. I don't wan - na

122

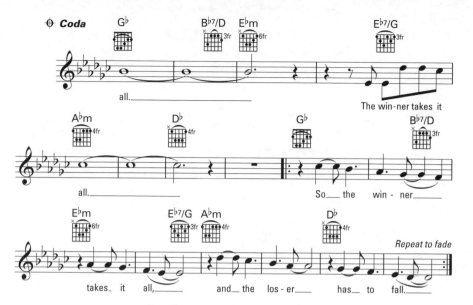

Verse 2:
I was in your arms thinking I belonged there
I figured it made sense, building me a fence
Building me a home, thinking I'd be strong there
But I was a fool playing by the rules
The gods may throw the dice, their minds as cold as ice
And someone way down here loses someone dear.

The winner take it all, the loser has to fall
It's simple and it's plain, why should I complain?

Verse 3:
But tell me does she kiss like I used to kiss you?
Does it feel the same when she calls your name?
Somewhere deep inside you must know I miss you
But what can I say, rules must be obeyed
The judges will decide, the likes of me abide
Spectators of the show always staying low.

The game is on again, a lover or a friend
A big thing or a small, the winner takes it all.

Verse 4:
I don't wanna talk if it makes you feel sad
And I understand you've come to shake my hand
I apologise if it makes you feel bad
Seeing me so tense, no self-confidence
But you see, the winner takes it all
The winner takes it all.

Ghost Town

Words & Music by Jerry Dammers

© Copyright 1981 Plangent Visions Music Limited.
All Rights Reserved. International Copyright Secured.

1. This town (town_____) is com-ing like a ghost town.
(Verse 2 see block lyrics)

All the clubs____ are be-ing closed down._____

This place (town_____) is com-ing like a ghost town.

Bands won't play no more. Too much fight-ing on the dance floor.

Verse 2:
This town is coming like a ghost town
Why must the youth fight against themself
Goverment's leaving the youths on the shelf
This place is coming like a ghost town
No job to be found in this country
Can't go on no more, the people getting angry.

La la la la la *etc.*

125

Under Pressure

Words & Music by David Bowie, Freddie Mercury, Roger Taylor, John Deacon & Brian May

© Copyright 1981 Tintoretto Music/RZO Music Limited (42%)/
EMI Music Publishing Limited (8%)/
Queen Music Limited (50%).
All Rights Reserved. International Copyright Secured.

♩ = 120

(Both Voices) Pres - sure, push - ing down__ on me,__ press - ing down__ on you__ no man ask for. Un - der pres-sure that burns a build - ing down, splits a fam-'ly in two,__ puts peo-ple on streets._ Boom bah bah bay, boom bah bah bay, do day dah, do day dah. That's O. K. (Voice 1) That's the ter-ror of know - ing what this world is a-bout. Watch-ing some good friends scream-ing "Let me out!" Pray to-

126

-mor - row___ takes me high - er, pres-sure on peo - ple, peo-ple

on streets. Do do do. Ba da ba ba ba.

O. K.___ *(Voice 2)* Chip-ping a - round,___

___ kick my brains round the floor. These are the days___ it nev-er rains but it pours.___

___ Ee do day doh, ee da bo ba bop. Mm da bop,

bay dop! *(V1)* Peo-ple on streets. *(V2)* De de dee do day.

(V1) Peo-ple on streets. *(V2)* De de dee do dee do dee do. *(V1)* It's the

Come On Eileen

Words & Music by Kevin Rowland, James Paterson & Kevin Adams

© Copyright EMI Music Publishing Limited (80%)/
Kevin Adams Music Limited (20%).
All Rights Reserved. International Copyright Secured.

1. Poor old John-ny Ray_____ sound-ed

sad up-on_ the ra-di-o_ moved a mill-ion hearts in mo-no.

Our moth-ers cried,_ sang a-long, who'd blame_ them?

2. These peo-ple round here_ wear beat-en down eyes, sunk in smoke dried faces they're re-

You've grown, *(you're grown up)* so grown, *(so grown up).* Now_

-signed to what their fate is. But not us, *(no nev-er.)* No, not us *(no nev-er).* We_

___ I must say more_ than ev-er. *(Come on_ Ei-leen))*

___ are far too young and clev-er. *(Re-mem-ber))*

Too-ra, too-ra, too-ra, loo-rye_ aye. { And we can
{ Ei-leen I'll

131

Should I Stay Or Should I Go

Words & Music by Joe Strummer & Mick Jones

© Copyright 1982 Nineden Limited/Universal Music Publishing Limited.
All rights in Germany administered by Universal Music Publ. GmbH.
All Rights Reserved. International Copyright Secured.

1. Darl - ing, you've got to let me know, should I stay or should I go?

(Verse 2 see block lyrics)

If you say that you are mine, I'll be here till the end of time. So you've got to let me know,

1. should I stay or should I go? 2. It's al-ways tease, tease,

2. Should I stay or should I go now? Should I stay or should I

134

135

Verse 2:
It's always tease, tease, tease
You're happy when I'm on my knees
One day it's fine and next it's black
So if you want me off your back
Well, come on and let me know
Should I stay or should I go?

Karma Chameleon

Words & Music by George O'Dowd, Jonathan Moss, Roy Hay, Michael Craig & Philip Pickett

© Copyright 1983 EMI/Virgin Music (Publishers) Limited (80%)/
BMG Music Publishing Limited (20%).
All Rights Reserved. International Copyright Secured.

♩ = 184

1. There's a lov-ing in_ your eyes_ all_ the way.___ If__ I__
(Verse 2 see block lyrics)

lis - ten to__ your lies,___ would you say? I'm_ a man

with - out__ con - vic - tion,_ I'm_ a man_ who does - n't

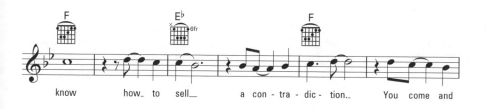

know how_ to sell_ a con - tra - dic - tion._ You come and

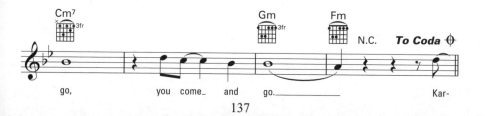

go, you come_ and go.___ Kar-

137

- ma, kar- ma, kar- ma, kar- ma, kar- ma cham - e - le - on,

you come and go, you come_ and go._____

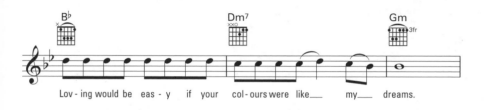

Lov - ing would be eas - y if your col - ours were like___ my___ dreams.

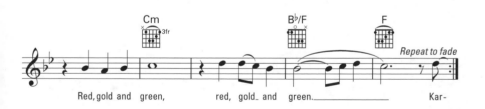

Repeat to fade

Red, gold and green, red, gold_ and green._____ Kar-

Verse 2:
Didn't hear your wicked words every day
And you used to be so sweet, I heard you say
That my love was an addiction
When we cling, our love is strong
When you go, you're gone forever
You string along, you string along.

Young At Heart

Words & Music by Robert Hodgens, Siobhan Fahey & Bobby Valentino

© Copyright 1982 Universal/Anxious Music Limited (55%)/
Hornall Brothers Music Limited (25%)/
Reverb Music Limited (20%).
All Rights Reserved. International Copyright Secured.

Verse 2:
Young at heart yet not a chance to be a child at all
They told us tales, they told us lies
Don't they know they shouldn't have told us at all?

True

Words & Music by Gary Kemp

© Copyright 1983 Reformation Publishing Company Limited.
All Rights Reserved. International Copyright Secured.

1. So true,— fun-ny how it seems— al-ways in time, but

(Verse 2 see block lyrics)

nev - er in line for dreams.— Head o - ver heels— when toe to toe,

— this is the sound— of my soul,— this is the sound.—

I bought a tick-et to the world,— but now I've come back a - gain.—

To Coda

Why do I find it hard to write the next line?— When

I want the truth to be said...—

142

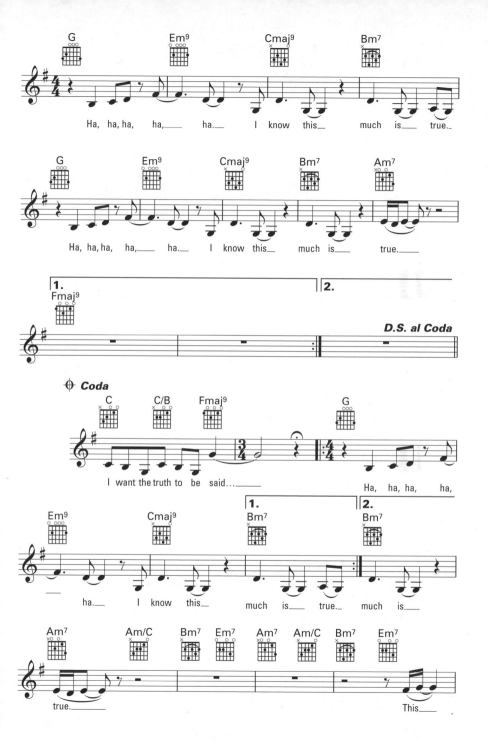

Verse 2:
With a thrill in my head and a pill on my tongue
Dissolve the nerves that have just begun
Listening to Marvin all night long
This is the sound of my soul, this is the sound.

Always slipping from my hands
Sand's a time of its own
Take your seaside arms and write the next line
Oh, I want the truth to be known…
Ha, ha, ha, ha, ha. I know this much is true
Ha, ha, ha, ha, ha. I know this much is true.

The Power Of Love

Words & Music by Holly Johnson, Mark O'Toole, Peter Gill & Brian Nash

© Copyright 1984 Perfect Songs Limited.
All Rights Reserved. International Copyright Secured.

Hello

Words & Music by Lionel Richie

© Copyright 1983, 1984 Brockman Music (ASCAP)/Brenda Richie Publishing (ASCAP).
Universal Music Publishing Limited (50%) (administered in Germany by Universal Music Publ. GmbH)/
Kobalt Music Publishing Limited (50%).
All Rights Reserved. International Copyright Secured.

Am   Bm⁷   C⁶   Bm⁷   Dm   G

arms are op - en wide._   'Cause you know just what to say,   and you

C   F   B♭   Eaug   E

know just what to do._____   And I   want to tell_ you so_____ much   "I love

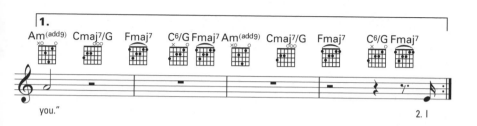

1.
Am⁽ᵃᵈᵈ⁹⁾ Cmaj⁷/G Fmaj⁷   C⁶/G Fmaj⁷ Am⁽ᵃᵈᵈ⁹⁾ Cmaj⁷/G   Fmaj⁷   C⁶/G Fmaj⁷

you."   2. I

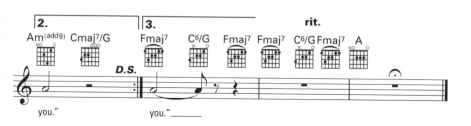

2.   **3.**   **rit.**
Am⁽ᵃᵈᵈ⁹⁾ Cmaj⁷/G   Fmaj⁷   C⁶/G   Fmaj⁷ Fmaj⁷   C⁶/G Fmaj⁷   A

                D.S.

you."   you."_____

Verse 2:

I long to see the sunlight in your hair

And tell you time and time again how much I care

Sometimes I feel my heart will overflow

Hello I've just got to let you know

(2 & 3°)

'Cause I wonder where you are

And I wonder what you do

Are you somewhere feeling lonely

Or is someone loving you?

Tell me how to win your heart

For I haven't got a clue

But let me start by saying "I love you."

Easy Lover

Words by Phil Collins • Music by Phil Collins, Nathan East & Philip Bailey

© Copyright 1984 Philip Collins Limited/New East Music/Sir And Trini Music.
Hit & Run Music (Publishing) Limited (50%)/
Notting Hill Music (UK) Limited (25%)/
Universal Music Publishing MGB Limited (25%).
All Rights in Germany Administered by Musik Edition Discoton GmbH (A Division of Universal Music Publishing Group).
All Rights Reserved. International Copyright Secured.

She will play___ a-round and leave you, leave___ you and de-ceive you.

Bet-ter for - get___ it. Oh,___ you'll re - gret it.___

No, you'll nev-er change her, so leave her, leave her. Get out quick 'cause

see-ing is be-liev-ing. It's the on - ly way_ you'll ev - er know___

1.

2.

D.S. to fade

she's___ an ea - sy lov - ___ an ea - sy lov -

Verse 2:
You're the one that wants to hold her
Hold her and control her
Better forget it, you'll never get it
'Cause she'll say that there's no other
Till she find another
Better forget it, oh, you'll regret it
And don't try to change her
Just leave her, leave her
You're not the only one
And seeing is believing
It's the only way you'll ever know.

151

I Want To Know What Love Is

Words & Music by Mick Jones

© Copyright 1984 Somerset Songs Publishing Incorporated, USA.
All Rights Reserved. International Copyright Secured.

1. I've got-ta take a lit - tle time,___ a lit-tle time to think_ things

(Verses 2 & 3 see block lyrics)

o - ver. I'd bet-ter read be-tween the lines___ in case I

need it when I'm old-er.___

In my life___ there's been heart-ache and pain,___

I don't know___ if I can face_ it a-gain, can't stop now I've

tra-velled so far___ to change this lone - ly life.___

I want to know what love is,____   I want you to show

____ me.   I want to feel what love is,____   I know you can show__

To Coda   **D.C. al Coda**

____ me.____

Coda

I want to know what love is,____   I want you to show__ me.

Repeat to fade

I want to feel what love is,____   I know you can show__ me._____

Verse 2:
Up this mountain I must climb
Feels like the world up on my shoulder
Through the clouds I see love shine
It keeps me warm as life grows colder.

Vere 3:
I'm gonna take a little time
A little time to look around me
I've got no where left to hide
It looks like life has finally found me.

153

Don't Turn Around

Words & Music by Albert Hammond & Diane Warren

© Copyright 1985 Albert Hammond Enterprises Incorporated/Editions Sunset Publishing Incorporated/Realsongs, USA.
Windswept Music (London) Limited (50%)/
EMI Music Publishing Limited (33.33%)/
BMG Music Publishing Limited (16.67%).
All Rights Reserved. International Copyright Secured.

154

door,   see if I care,___   go on and go___ now.___   But

Bmaj⁷

E

don't turn a - round,   'cause you're gon - na   see   my   heart break -

C♯m⁷   **F♯11**   **Bmaj⁷**

- ing.   Don't   turn   a - round,   I   don't want you

E   **F♯11**   **Bmaj⁷**

see - ing me cry - ing.   Just walk a - way,   it's tear-ing me a -

E   **C♯m⁷**   **F♯11**

- part   that   you're   leav   -   ing.   I'm   let - ting   you   go___

A   **F♯11**

To Coda ⊕

and   I   won't let   you   know.___

1.

Bmaj⁷   **E**   **F♯11**

___   Ba - by,   I   won't let   you   know.___

155

it's tear-ing me a - part that you're leav - ing. I'm let-ting you go.

D.S. al Coda

Don't turn a - round,

Coda

Don't you__ turn a - round. Uh uh, I don't

want you to see me cry - ing.___ (Don't turn a- round,) Hey, hey don't you

Repeat to fade

turn a - round when you're leav - ing.___ (Don't turn a - round,)

Verse 2:
I won't miss your arms around me
Holding me tight
And if you ever think about me
Just know that I'm gonna be alright
I'm gonna be strong, I'm gonna be fine
Don't worry about this heart of mine
I know I'll survive, I'll make it through
And I'll learn to live without you.

157

The Sun Always Shines On TV

Words & Music by Pal Waaktaar

© Copyright 1985 ATV Music Limited.
Sony/ATV Music Publishing (UK) Limited.
All Rights Reserved. International Copyright Secured.

♩ = 124

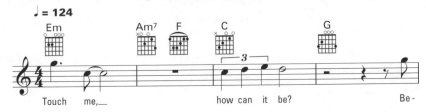

Touch me,— how can it be? Be-

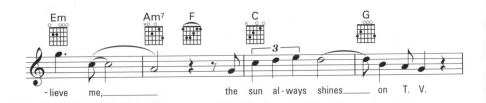

-lieve me,——— the sun al-ways shines——— on T. V.

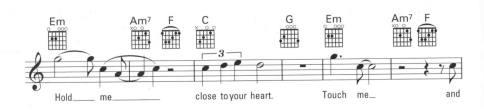

Hold— me——— close to your heart. Touch me— and

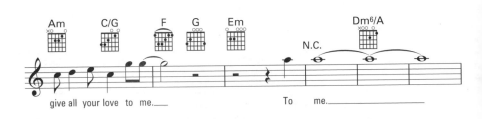

give all your love to me.— To me.———

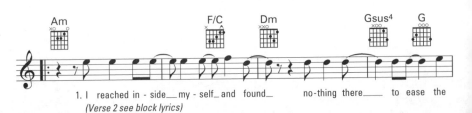

1. I reached in-side— my-self— and found— no-thing there——— to ease the

(Verse 2 see block lyrics)

158

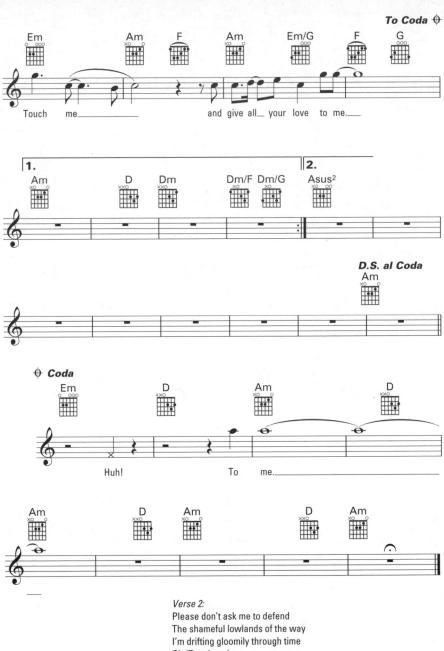

Verse 2:
Please don't ask me to defend
The shameful lowlands of the way
I'm drifting gloomily through time
Oh (Touch me)
I reached myself today
Thinking there's got to be some way
To keep my troubles distant.

Eternal Flame

Words & Music by Susanna Hoffs, Tom Kelly & Billy Steinberg

© Copyright 1988 & 1989 Billy Steinberg Music/Sony/ATV Tunes LLC/Bangophile Music, USA.
Sony/ATV Music Publishing (UK) Limited (66.66%)/
Universal Music Publishing Limited (33.34%).
All rights in Germany administered by Universal Music Publ. GmbH.
All Rights Reserved. International Copyright Secured.

1. Close your eyes, give me your hand dar-ling. Do you feel_ my heart beat
(Verse 2 see block lyrics)

- ing, do you un-der-stand?____ Do you feel the same,___ am I on-ly

1. dream - ing? Is this burn-ing an e-tern-al flame? **2.** dream - ing? Or

is this burn - ing__ an e-ter-nal flame?____ Say my name,

sun shines through the rain.____ A whole life so lone-ly,____ and then you

come and ease the pain. I don't want to lose this feel - ing, oh.____

161

—(Guitar)

Say my name,   sun shines through the rain.___ A whole life   so lone-ly,___ and then you

come and   ease the pain.   I don't want to lose this   feel - ing,   oh.

3. Close your eyes,___ give me your hand.___   Do you feel___ my heart beat -

- ing,   do you un-der-stand?___ Do you feel the same,___   am I on-ly

dream - ing?   Or   is   this   burn - ing___   an   e - ter - nal   flame?___

Verse 2:
I believe it's meant to be darling
I watch you when you are sleeping
You belong with me
So you feel the same, am I only dreaming
Or is this burning an eternal flame?

163

La Bamba

Traditional

Adapted & Arranged by Ritchie Valens

© Copyright 1958 Kemo Music Company, USA.
Carlin Music Corporation.
All Rights Reserved. International Copyright Secured.

♩ = 157

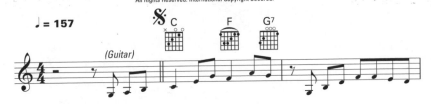

(Guitar)

Pa - ra bai - lar la bam - ba, para bai - lar la bam-

- ba, se ne - ce - si'___ u - na po - ca de gra - ci - a. U - na po - ca de

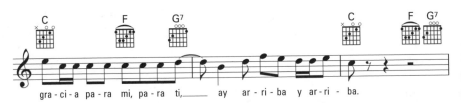

gra - ci - a pa - ra mi, pa - ra ti,___ ay ar - ri - ba y ar - ri - ba.

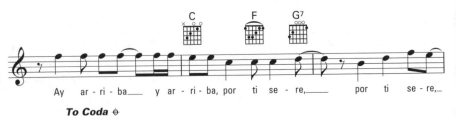

Ay ar - ri - ba___ y ar - ri - ba, por ti se - re,___ por ti se - re,

To Coda ⊕

___ por ti se - re.___ Yo no soy ma - ri - ne - ro, yo no soy ma - ri-

164

China In Your Hand

Words & Music by Carol Decker & Ronald Rogers

© Copyright 1987 Media International 5 Limited.
BMG Music Publishing Limited.
All Rights Reserved. International Copyright Secured.

Verse 2:
Come from greed never born of the seed
Took a life from a barren land
Oh, eyes wide like a child in the form of man
A prophesy for a fantasy
The curse of a vivid mind.

167

Never Gonna Give You Up

Words & Music by Mike Stock, Matt Aitken & Pete Waterman

© Copyright 1987 Universal Music Publishing Limited (33.34%)/Sony/ATV Music Publishing (UK) Limited (33.33%)/All Boys Music Limited (33.33%).
All rights in Germany administered by Universal Music Publ. GmbH.
All Rights Reserved. International Copyright Secured.

1. We're no stran-gers to love___ you know the rules and so do I.___
(Verses 2 & 3 see block lyrics)

A full com-mit-ment's what I'm think-ing of___ you would-n't get this from

a -ny oth-er guy. I___ just wan-na tell you how I'm feel-ing, got-ta make you

un-der stand. Nev-er gon-na give you_ up,_ nev-er gon-na let you_ down,_ nev-er gon-na

run a - round_ and de - sert you. Nev-er gon-na make you_ cry,_ nev-er gon-na

say good- bye,___ nev-er gon-na tell a lie___ and hurt_ you.

Verses 2 & 3:
We've known each other for so long
Your heart's been aching, but you're too shy to say it
Inside we both know what's been going on
We know the game and we're gonna play it
And if you ask me how I'm feeling
Don't tell me you're too blind to see.

Perfect

Words & Music by Mark E. Nevin

© Copyright 1988 MCA Music Limited.
Universal/MCA Music Limited.
All rights in Germany administered by Universal/MCA Music Publ. GmbH.
All Rights Reserved. International Copyright Secured.

1.I don't want _____ half-heart-ed love af-fairs. _____

(Verses 2 & 3 see block lyrics)

I need_ some - one_ who_____ real-ly cares.

Life_ is too_ short_____ to play sil - ly games,_____

I've prom-ised my - self____ I won't do_ that a - gain.

It's___ got to be_____ per - fect.____

It's___ got to be_____ worth it,_ yeah.

Verses 2 & 3:
Young hearts are foolish, they make such mistakes
They're much too eager to give their love away
Well I have been foolish too many times
Now I'm determined I'm gonna get it right.

Like A Prayer

Words & Music by Madonna & Pat Leonard

© Copyright 1989 Webo Girl Publishing Incorporated/Bleu Disque Music Company Incorporated/Johnny Yuma Music/Orangejello Music, USA.
Warner/Chappell Music Publishing Limited (50%)/
EMI Music Publishing Limited (25%)/
Sony/ATV Music Publishing (UK) Limited (25%).
All Rights Reserved. International Copyright Secured.

there. 1. I hear your voice,___ it's like an an - gel sigh - ing.
(Verse 2 see block lyrics)

I have no choice,___ I hear your voice, feels like fly - ing.

I close my eyes.___ Oh God, I think I'm fall - ing

out of the sky. I close my eyes. Hea - ven help me.

When you call my__ name__ it's like a lit - tle__ prayer.__ I'm down on my__ knees,__

__ I wan-na take you there. In the mid - night_ hour__ I can feel__ your pow-

1.
- er just like a___ prayer.__ You know I'll take you

2.
___ You know I'll take you

173

there. When you call my_ name_ it's like a lit - tle prayer._ I'm down on my_ knees,_
there. In the mid-night hour_ I can feel your pow - er just like a_ prayer._

_ I wan-na take you there.
_You know I'll take you

Life is a mys - te - ry._

_ Ev-'ry-one must stand a - lone._ I hear you call my name_

_ and it feels like home. Just like a prayer your voice can take me there,

just like a muse to me._ You are a mys-te-ry._ Just like a dream,

you are not what you_ seem._ Just like a prayer, no choice, your voice can take me

174

Verse 2:
Like a child you whisper softly to me
You're in control
Just like a child, now I'm dancing
It's like a dream, no end and no beginning
You're here with me, it's like a dream
Let the choir sing.

The 1990s

Large egos dominated the No. 1 slot of the 1990s: Elton John & George Michael duetted, Madonna, Britney Spears, Whitney Houston and Michael Jackson didn't, but all rang the No. 1 bell. So did Bryan Adams and Céline Dion who each recorded a song featured in a blockbuster movie and were consequently rewarded with huge commercial success worldwide as the legends of Robin Hood and The Titanic were once more retold for the cinema. The Troggs' 'Love Is All Around', a hit back in 1967, got a new lease of life from Wet Wet Wet and meanwhile Oasis scored their first No. 1 with 'Some Might Say'. Madonna took an experimental step with her single 'Frozen' which featured eastern-flavoured strings and percussion on a bed of electronics; it was critically acclaimed as one of her more interesting records and the buying public thought so too.

Some Might Say

Words & Music by Noel Gallagher

© Copyright 1995 Oasis Music/Creation Songs Limited.
Sony/ATV Music Publishing (UK) Limited.
All Rights Reserved. International Copyright Secured.

1. Some might say__ that sun-shine fol-lows thun-der
(Verse 2 see block lyrics)

go and tell____ it to__ the man____ who can-not shine.____

__ Some might say__ that we should ne-ver pon-

- der on our thoughts____ to-day__ 'cause they

__ hold sway__ ov-er time.__ Some might say__

__ we will find__ a bright-er day.____

Some might say_____ we will find a bright-er__ day.__

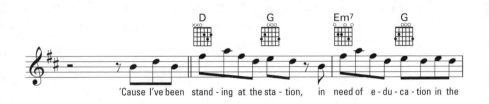

'Cause I've been stand-ing at the sta - tion, in need of e - du - ca - tion in the

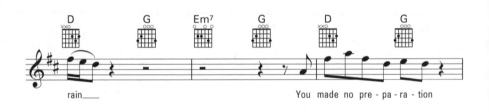

rain__ You made no pre - pa - ra - tion

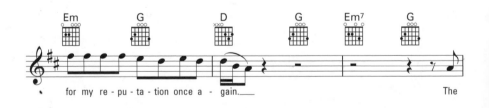

for my re - pu - ta - tion once a - gain.__ The

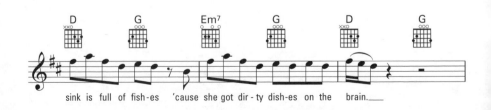

sink is full of fish-es 'cause she got dir - ty dish-es on the brain.__

It was ov-er-flow-ing gent-ly but it's all e-le-men-tary my
2° And my dog's been itch-ing, itch-ing in the kitch-en once a-

1.

friend._____
-gain._____

2.

Some might say,___

some might say.___
You know what some might say,___

you know what some might say.___

Verse 2:
Some might say they don't believe in heaven
Go and tell it to the man who lives in hell
Some might say you get what you've been given
If you don't get yours I won't get mine as well.

179

Nothing Compares 2 U

Words & Music by Prince

© Copyright 1985 Controversy Music, USA.
Universal/MCA Music Limited.
All rights in Germany administered by Universal/MCA Music Publ. GmbH.
All Rights Reserved. International Copyright Secured.

1. It's been se - ven hours and fif - teen days

(Verses 2-3. see block lyrics)

since U took your love a - way.

I go out ev - 'ry night and sleep all day

since U took your love a - way.

Since U been gone I can do what-ev -

- er I want.

I can see whom-ev - er I choose.

I can eat my din-ner in a fan-cy res-tau-rant but

Verse 2:

It's been so lonely without U here, like a bird without a wing
Nothing can stop these lonely tears from falling, tell me baby, where did I go wrong?
I could put my arms around ev'ry boy I see
But they'd only remind me of U
I went 2 the doctor and guess what he told me, guess what he told me?
He said "Girl, U better try 2 have fun, don't matter what U do", but he's a fool.

Verse 3:
Instrumental
All the flowers that I planted, Mama, in the backyard
All died when U went away
I know that living with U, baby, was sometimes hard
But I'm willing 2 give it another try.

Show Me Heaven

Words & Music by Maria McKee, Jay Rifkin & Eric Rackin

© Copyright 1990 Famous Music LLC/Ensign Music Corporation, USA.
Sony/ATV Music Publishing (UK) Limited.
All Rights Reserved. International Copyright Secured.

1. There you go, flash-ing fe - ver from your eyes.
(Verse 2 see block lyric)

Hey babe, come ov - er here_ and shut down tight._

I'm not de-ny - ing we're fly-ing a - bove_

_ it all,_ hold my hand don't let me fall_

you've such a-ma - zing grace, I've ne - ver felt this way._

182

Oh,___ show me hea - ven, co - ver__ me,___
leave me breath - less.__ Oh,_____ show me hea - ven
please. If you know what it's like__ to dream a dream,
ba - by hold me tight and let__ this__ be.__ Oh,_____ Oh,___
show me hea - ven,__ co - ver__ me,___ leave me breath - less.__
Oh,_____ show me hea - ven please.

Repeat to fade

Verse 2:
Here I go, I'm shaking just like the breeze
Hey babe, I need your hand to steady me
I'm not denying I'm frightened as much as you
Though I'm barely touching you
I've shivers down my spine, and it feels divine.

(Everything I Do) I Do It For You
(from Robin Hood, Prince Of Thieves)

Words by Bryan Adams
Music by Robert John 'Mutt' Lange & Michael Kamen

© Copyright 1991 Almo Music Corporation/Out Of Pocket Productions Limited/Zachary Creek Music Incorporated/Miracle Creek Music Incorporated/2855 Music, USA.
Fintage Publishing And Collection (62.5%)/Imagem London Limited (18.75%)/
Universal Music Publishing Limited (18.75%) (administered in Germany by Universal Music Publ. GmbH).
All Rights Reserved. International Copyright Secured.

1. Look in-to my eyes, _____ you will see _____
(Verse 2 see block lyrics)

what you mean to _____ me. Search your heart, _____ search your

soul, _____ and when you find me there you'll search _____ no more. Don't

tell me it's not worth fight-ing for, you can't tell me it's not worth dy-ing

for. _____ You know it's true, _____ ev-'ry-thing I do, _____ I do it for

1.   **2.**

you.   There's no love _____ like

Verse 2:
Look into your heart, you will find
There's nothing there to hide
Take me as I am, take my life
I would give it all, I would sacrifice.

Don't Let The Sun Go Down On Me

Words & Music by Elton John & Bernie Taupin

© Copyright 1974 HST Management Limited/Rouge Booze Incorporated.
Universal Music Publishing Limited.
All rights administered in Germany by Universal Music Publ. GmbH.
All Rights Reserved. International Copyright Secured.

1. I can't light no more of your dark - ness.

All my pic-tures seem to fade to black and white.

I'm grow-ing tired and time stands still be - fore me.

Fro-zen here on the lad - der of my life.

Too late to save my-self from fall - ing.
(Verse 2 see block lyrics)

I took a chance and changed your way of life.

But you mis-read my mean-ing when I met___ you, closed the door and left me___ blind - ed by___ the light.___

Don't let the sun___ go down on me.___ Al-though I search my-self, it's al-ways some-one else I see.___ I'd just al-low a frag-ment of your life___ to wan-der free___

___ but los-ing ev - 'ry-thing___ is like the sun go - ing down on___ me.

D.S. al Fine
Fine

Verse 2:
I can't find the right romantic line
But see me once and see the way I feel
Don't discard me just because you think I mean you harm
But these cuts I have, they need love to help them heal.

187

I Will Always Love You

Words & Music by Dolly Parton

© Copyright 1975 Velvet Apple Music USA.
Carlin Music Corporation.
All Rights Reserved. International Copyright Secured.

Slowly, freely

If___ I_____ should_ stay,___ I___ would

on - ly_ be_ in___ your way._____ So I'll___

go,_____ but I__ know___ I'll__ think of you_ ev'ry step of the way.__

And I_____ will al-ways   love you,_____   will_ al-ways

poco accel.

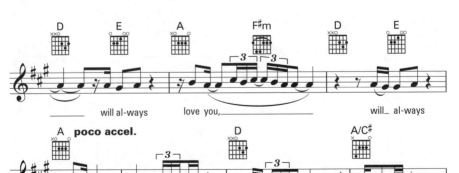

love you_____   you,_____   my darl-ing you,_

189

190

B   G#m   E   F#

___ you,_____ I   I will al - ways love you.___

B   G#m   E   F#

_____ I will al - ways   love___

B   G#m   E   rit.   F#

___ you,_____ I, I will al - ways   love___

N.C.

_____ you,___

E   B/D#

___ you._____ Darl-ing I love___ you.___   Ooh___ I'll

F#sus4   F#   Bsus2

al - ways I'll___ al - ways___   love___ you.

Love Is All Around

Words & Music by Reg Presley

© Copyright 1967 Dick James Music Limited.
Universal/Dick James Music Limited.
All rights in Germany administered by Universal Music Publ. GmbH.
All Rights Reserved. International Copyright Secured.

1. I feel it in my fin-gers I feel it in my toes.___ The

(Verse 2 see block lyrics)

love that's all a-round me and so the feel-ing grows.__ It's

writ-ten in the wind, it's ev-'ry-where I go.___ So

if you real-ly love me, come on and let it show.___

You know I love you, I al-ways will,___ my mind's made up by the

way that I feel.___ There's no be-gin-ning, there'll be no___ end,___ 'cause

on my__ love__ you can de - pend._____

Got to keep it mov - ing. It's

writ-ten in__the wind,__ oh,_____ ev-'ry-where I go.__ So

if you real - ly love me, come on and let it show._____ Come on and let

Repeat to fade

show.)
Come on and let__ it, come on and let__ it, come on and let__ it__ show.

Verse 2:
I see your face before me as I lay on my bed
I kinda get to thinking of all the things you said
You gave your promise to me, and I gave mine to you
I need someone beside me, in everything I do.

The Most Beautiful Girl In The World

Words & Music by Prince

© Copyright 1994 Controversy Music, USA.
Universal/MCA Music Limited.
All rights in Germany administered by Universal/MCA Music Publ. GmbH.
All Rights Reserved. International Copyright Secured.

♩ = 94

Could U be_____ the most beau -

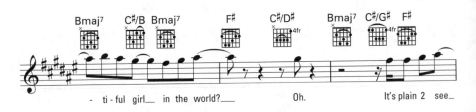

- ti - ful girl_ in the world?_____ Oh. It's plain 2 see_

_ U're the rea - son that God_ made a girl._____ Mm._

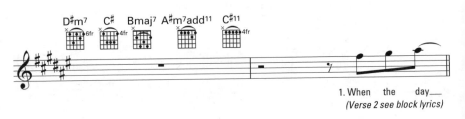

1. When the day_
(Verse 2 see block lyrics)

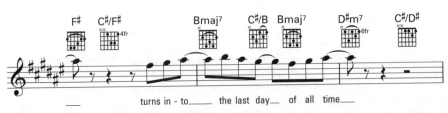

_ turns in - to_____ the last day_ of all time_

194

(So beau - ti - ful,___ beau - ti - ful.)_____ It's plain 2 see_

___ (plain 2 see)___ U're the rea - son that God__ made a girl._

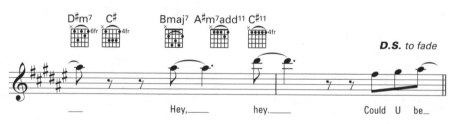

D#m⁷ C# Bmaj⁷ A#m⁷add¹¹ C#¹¹

D.S. to fade

___ Hey,___ hey.___ Could U be_

Verse 2:
How can I
Get through days when I can't get through hours
I can try
But when I do, I see U and I'm devoured, oh, yes
Who'd allow, who'd allow
A face 2 be soft as a flower
I could bow
And feel proud in the light of this power
Oh… yes…

197

You Are Not Alone

Words & Music by Robert Kelly

© Copyright 1995 Zomba Songs Incorporated, USA.
Zomba Music Publishers Limited.
All Rights Reserved. International Copyright Secured.

198

I am here to stay,___ but you are not___ a-lone___

but I am here___ with you,___ though we're far___ a-part,___

you're al-ways in___ my heart___ but you are not___ a-lone___

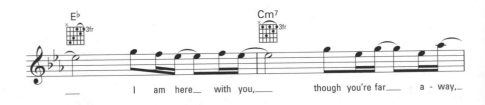

I am here___ with you,___ though you're far___ a-way,___

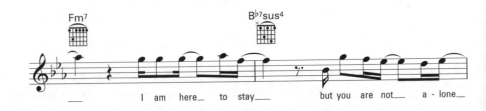

I am here___ to stay___ but you are not___ a-lone___

but I am here with you, though we're far a-part,

you're al-ways in my heart, you are not a-lone.

(*Spoken*) You are not alone...
You just reach out for me girl... in the morning in the
Together...

you are not alone... not alone.
evening not alone... not alone... you and me, not alone...

Repeat ad lib. to fade

Verse 2:
You are not alone
I am here with you
Though you're far away
I am here to stay
You are not alone
I am here with you
Though we're far apart
You're always in my heart
But you are not alone.

Verse 3:
Just the other night
I thought I heard you cry
Asking me to go
And hold you in my arms
I can hear your breaths
Your burdens I will bear
But first I need you here
Then forever can begin.

Verse 4:
You are not alone
I am here with you
Though you're far away
I am here to stay
But you are not alone
I am here with you
Though we're far apart
You're always in my heart
But you are not alone.

201

Don't Speak

Words & Music by Eric Stefani & Gwen Stefani

© Copyright 1996 Knock Yourself Out Music, USA.
Universal/MCA Music Limited.
All rights in Germany administered by Universal/MCA Music Publ. GmbH.
All Rights Reserved. International Copyright Secured.

♩ = 80

You and me ___ we used to be ___ to - geth - er,
ev-'ry day ___ to-geth-er, al - ways. I real-ly feel ___ that I'm
los - ing my best ___ friend, I can't be - lieve ___ this could ___ be the ___
___ end. It looks ___ as though ___ you're ___ let-ting go, ___ and
we die ___ both ___ you and I ___
if it's real ___ then I ___ don't want ___ to know. ___
with my head in my hands I'll soon be cry - ing.)

202

Don't speak, I know just what you're say - ing, so please stop ex-plain-
- ing, don't tell me 'cause it hurts.

Don't speak, I know what you're think - ing I don't need your rea-

1.
- sons, don't tell me 'cause it hurts. Old

me-mo-ries, they can be in-vit-ing but some are

all to-geth-er might-y fright-'ning as

2.
It's all end-ing, we've got to

203

204

...Baby One More Time

Words & Music by Max Martin

© Copyright 1998 Imagem London Limited.
All Rights Reserved. International Copyright Secured.

Oh ba - by, ba - by.

1. Oh ba - by, ba - by how was I sup - posed to know____ that
(Verse 2 see block lyrics)

some - thing was - n't right here? Oh ba - by, ba - by I should - n't have let____ you go.____

And now you're out of sight yeah. Show me how you want it

to be, Tell me ba - by 'cause I need to know now oh, be - cause.____

My lone - li - ness is kill - ing me and____ I,_____ I must con - fess I

still be - lieve,___ still be - lieve.___ When I'm not with you I lose my mind. Give me a sign,___

1.
hit me ba - by one more time.

2.
hit me ba - by one more time.

Oh ba - by, ba - by. Oh ba - by, ba - by, how

was I sup - posed to know?___

Oh, pret - ty ba - by, I should-n't have let___ you go.___

___ I must con - fess___ that my lone - li - ness___ is kill-ing me now,___

___ don't you know I___ still___ be - lieve___ that you will be here.

Verse 2:
Oh baby, baby the reason I breath is you
Boy, you got me blinded
Oh pretty baby there's nothing that I wouldn't do
It's not the way I planned it.

I Believe I Can Fly

Words & Music by R Kelly

© Copyright 1997 Zomba Songs Incorporated, USA
Imagem Music
All Rights Reserved. International Copyright Secured.

1. I used to think that I could not go on, and
(Verse 2 see block lyrics)

life was no - thing but an aw - ful song. But now I know the mean - ing of true

love I'm lean - ing on the ev - er - last - ing arms. If I can

see it, then I can do it, if I just be - lieve it, there's no - thing

to it. I be - lieve I can fly. I be - lieve I can touch the sky, I think a - bout it ev - 'ry

night and day, spread my wings and fly a - way, I be - lieve I can soar, see me run - ning through that

op - en door, I be - lieve I can fly, I be - lieve I can fly, I be - lieve I can

Verse 2:
See I was on the verge of breaking down
Sometimes silence can seem so loud
There are miracles in life I must achieve
But first I know it starts inside of me
If I can see it, then I can be it
If I just believe it, there's nothing to it.

My Heart Will Go On
(Love Theme from 'Titanic')

Words by Will Jennings • Music by James Horner

© Copyright 1997 Fox Film Music Corporation/TCF Music Publishing Incorporated (62.5%), USA/
Universal Music Publishing Limited (37.5%)
(administered in Germany by Universal Music Publ. GmbH).
All Rights Reserved. International Copyright Secured.

1. Ev - 'ry night in my dreams I see you, I feel_____you.
(Verse 2 see block lyrics)

That is how I know you go___ on.

Far a-cross the dis-tance and spa - ces be - tween____ us,

you have come to show you go on.

Near, far, wher - ev - er you are,___ I be -

- lieve that the heart does go___ on.

210

Verse 2:
Love can touch us one time and last for a lifetime
And never let go till we're gone
Love was when I loved you, one true time I hold you
In my life we'll always go on.

211

Frozen

Words & Music By Madonna & Patrick Leonard

© Copyright 1999 Webo Girl Publishing Incorporated, No Tomato Music & Lemonjello Music, USA.
Warner/Chappell Music Limited (50%)/
Sony/ATV Music Publishing (UK) Limited (25%)/
EMI Music Publishing Limited (25%).
All Rights Reserved. International Copyright Secured.

1. You on - ly see what your eyes want to see,
how can life be what you
(Verse 2 see block lyrics)

want it to be?_ You're fro - zen when your heart's not o - pen.

You're so con - sumed with how much you get._
You waste your time with
(Verse 3 see block lyrics)

hate and re - gret. You're bro - ken when your heart's not o - pen.

Verse 2:
Now there's no point in placing the blame
And you should know I suffer the same
If I lose you, my heart will be broken
Love is a bird, she needs to fly
Let all the hurt inside of you die
You're frozen when your heart's not open.

Verse 3:
You only see what your eyes want to see
How can life be what you want it to be?
You're frozen, when your heart's not open.

Flying Without Wings

Words & Music by Steve Mac & Wayne Hector

© Copyright 1999 Rokstone Music (50%)/
Rondor Music (London) Limited (50%).
All rights in Germany administered by Rondor Musikverlag GmbH.
All Rights Reserved. International Copyright Secured.

♩ = 73

N.C.

1. Ev-'ry-bo-dy's look-ing for that some-thing,

one thing that makes it all com-plete. You find it in___ the strang-est pla-

- ces,___ pla-ces you nev-er knew it could be.___

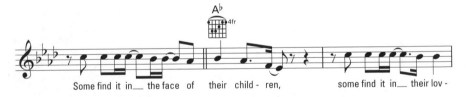

Some find it in___ the face of their child-ren, some find it in___ their lov-

-er's eyes. Who can de-ny___ the joy___ it brings___ when you've found that spe-cial

thing? You're fly-ing with-out wings. 2. Some find it shar-ing ev-'ry

morn-ing._____ Some in their so - li-ta - ry lives.
(Verse 3 see block lyrics)

You find it in__ the words of oth-ers,_____ a sim-ple line__ can make you

laugh_____ or_____ cry. You find it in the deep-est

friend-ships,_____ the kind__ you che-rish all___

your life,_____ and when you know how much that means, you've found that spe-cial

thing, you're fly-ing with-out wings._____ So, im-pos-si -

- ble_____ as they may seem_____ you've got to fight for ev-er-y__

To Coda ⊕

dream. 'Cause who's to know which one you___ let go would have made you___ com-

- plete._____ 3. Well,___ for me it's___ wak-ing up be-

D.S. al Coda

Coda

- thing. I'm fly-ing with-out wings. And you're the place my life be-gins,

___ and you'll be where it ends,___ I'm fly-ing with-out

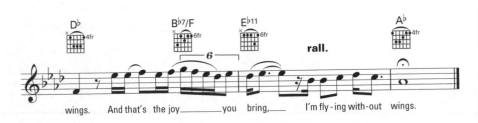

rall.

wings. And that's the joy_____you bring,___ I'm fly-ing with-out wings.

Verse 2:
Well, for me it's waking up beside you
To watch the sun rise on your face
To know that I can say I love you
In any given time or place
It's little things that only I know
Those are the things that make you mine
And it's like flying without wings
'Cause you're my special thing
I'm flying without wings

The 2000s

At the start of the 2000s Atomic Kitten hit the big time with their second single, 'Whole Again' which originally featured future tabloid star Kerry Katona but was later re-recorded to include her replacement Jenny Frost instead. Robbie Williams and Nicole Kidman re-made 'Somethin' Stupid', the lovers' duet that Frank Sinatra had once rather worryingly performed with his daughter Nancy, and what with Kylie Minogue, Christina Aguilera and Madonna all reaching No. 1,

the first half of the decade seemed to be reflecting a preoccupation with celebrity rather than musical innovation. The second half, though, started off with No. 1s from more exotic newcomers like Beirut-born Mika ('Grace Kelly'), Welsh soul singer Duffy ('Mercy') and Barbadian beauty queen Rihanna ('Umbrella'). Slow-burner of the decade was surely the Leonard Cohen song 'Hallelujah' which (despite versions by Jeff Buckley, Damien Rice, Rufus Wainwright and eventually pretty much everybody else) only finally planted its flag at the summit of the charts in 2008 courtesy of *X-Factor* winner Alexandra Burke. She was not even born when Columbia records declined to release Leonard Cohen's original studio version in 1984, calling it 'uncommercial'.

Beautiful Day

Words by Bono • Music by U2

© Copyright 2000 Blue Mountain Music Limited/Mother Music/PolyGram International Music Publishing Limited.
All rights in Germany administered by Universal Music Publ. GmbH.
All Rights Reserved. International Copyright Secured.

1. The heart is a bloom,____ shoots
(2.) but you've got

up through the sto - ny ground.____ But there's no room,____
____ no des - ti - na - tion. You're in the mud____

no space____ to rent in this town.____ You're out of luck,____
in the maze____ of her i - ma - gi - na - tion. You love this____

and the rea - son that you had to care.____
____ town,____ ev - en if it____ does-n't

____ The traf-fic is stuck,____ and you're not mov ing an y- where.__
ring true. You've been all ov - er, and it's____ been all ov-er you.

1° only

You thought you'd found____ a friend____

218

219

G   D   A

Fine

— I know I'm not— a hope-less— case.—

(A) (Bm) (D) (G) (D) (A)

(Guitar solo)

G^{add9}/E   D⁵

1. See the world in green and blue,— see Chi - na right—
2. See the Be -douin fires at night,— see the oil - fields

Dsus⁴   D   G^{add9}/E

— in front— of you. See the can - yons bro - ken by cloud.
at first light and, see the bird with a leaf in her mouth.

1.

D⁵

2.

Dsus⁴   D   A

3

See the tu - na fleets clear - ing the sea out. co - lours came out.
Af - ter the flood all the

N.C.

Day,— day,—

A⁵   B⁵   D⁵   G⁵

D.S. al Fine

— it was a beau - ti - ful— day.— Don't

220

Whole Again

Words & Music by Stuart Kershaw, Andy McCluskey, Bill Padley & Jeremy Godfrey

© Copyright 2000 EMI Virgin Music Limited (50%)/
Windswept Music (London) Limited (30%)/
Wise Buddah Music Limited/Universal Music Publishing Limited (20%).
All rights in Germany administered by Universal Music Publ. GmbH.
All Rights Reserved. International Copyright Secured.

1. If you see me walking down the street staring at the sky

and dragging my two feet, you just pass me by, it still makes me

cry, but you can make me whole again.

2. If you see me with another man, laughing and joking
(Verse 3 see block lyrics)

-ing, doing what I can, I won't put you down, 'cause I want you a-

-round, and you can make me whole again.

221

Verse 3:
Time is laying heavy on my heart
Seems I've got too much of it
Since we've been apart
My friends make me smile
If only for a while
You can make me whole again.

Somethin' Stupid

Words & Music by C. Carson Parks

© Copyright 1967 Greenwood Music Company, USA.
Montclare Music Company Limited.
All Rights Reserved. International Copyright Secured.

♩ = 104

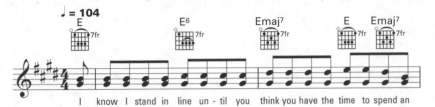

I know I stand in line un - til you think you have the time to spend an

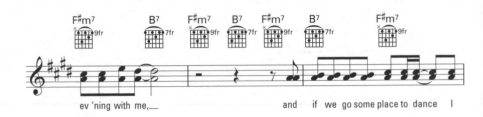

ev 'ning with me,___ and if we go some place to dance I

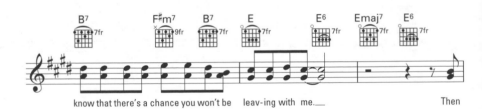

know that there's a chance you won't be leav-ing with me.___ Then

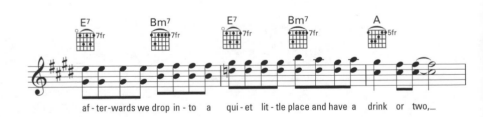

af - ter-wards we drop in - to a qui - et lit - tle place and have a drink or two,___

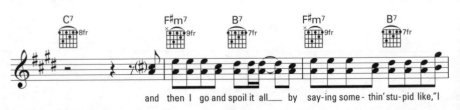

and then I go and spoil it all___ by say-ing some - thin' stu-pid like,"I

love you."_ I can see it in your eyes that you des-

-pise the same old lies you heard the night be-fore,_ and

though it's just a line to you,_ to me it's true and nev-er seemed_ so right be-fore._

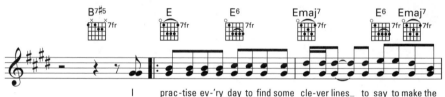

I prac-tise ev-'ry day to find some cle-ver lines_ to say to make the
(2° Instrumental until *)

mean-ing come true,_ but then I think I'll wait un-til the

B7   F#m7   B7   E   E6   Emaj7   E6   E

ev 'ning gets late and I'm a - lone with you.__

The
*

time is right, your per-fume fills my head, the stars get red and, oh, the

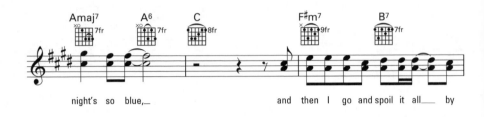

night's so blue,___ and then I go and spoil it all___ by

say - ing some - thin' stu - pid like, "I love you."___

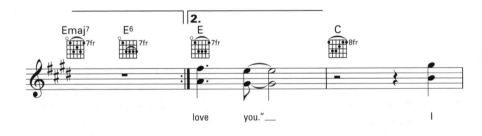

love you."___ I

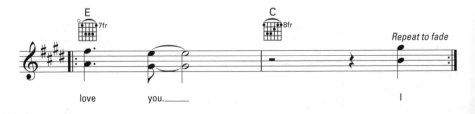

love you.___ I

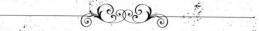

If You're Not The One

Words & Music by Daniel Bedingfield

© Copyright 2002 Sony/ATV Music Publishing (UK) Limited.
All Rights Reserved. International Copyright Secured.

1. If you're not the one then why does my soul feel glad today?
(Verse 2 see block lyrics)

If you're not the one then why does my hand fit yours

this way? If you are not mine then why does your heart return

my call? If you are not mine would I have the strength to stand at all?

I never know what the future brings, but I know you're here with me now. We'll make it through

and I hope you are the one I share my life with.

227

B♭add9   Cm⁷add¹¹   E♭sus²

___ If I'm not made_ for you_ then why___ does my heart tell___ me that I am?_

Gm⁷   F   Cm⁷   E♭9

___ Is there a-ny way_ that I___ can stay___ in your arms?_____ 'Cause I___

Gm   E♭   F   E♭   B♭

miss you,   bo-dy and soul so strong_____ that it takes_ my breath_ a-way. And I breathe_

Gm   E♭   F   E♭/B♭   B♭

___ you in-to my heart_ and_ pray_____ for the strength to stand to-day. 'Cause I love_

Gm   E♭   F   E♭/B♭   B♭

_____ you,_ whe-ther it's wrong or__ right_____ and though I can't be with you_ to-night_

E♭   F   B♭add9

D.S. al Fine

___ you know my heart is___ by your side. I don't wan-na run a-way_ but I_

Verse 2:
If I don't need you then why am I crying on my bed?
If I don't need you then why does your name resound in my head?
If you're not for me then why does this distance maim my life?
If you're not for me then why do I dream of you as my wife?
I dont know why you're so far away, but I know that this much is true
We'll make it through and I hope you are the one I share my life with.

229

Can't Get You Out Of My Head

Words & Music by Cathy Dennis & Rob Davis

© Copyright 2001 EMI Music Publishing Limited (50%)/
Universal/MCA Music Limited (50%) (administered in Germany by Universal/MCA Music Publ. GmbH).
All Rights Reserved. International Copyright Secured.

♩ = 126

La la la, la___ la la la la, la la la, la___ la la la la.

la la. I just can't get you out of my head. Boy, your

lov - ing is all I think a - bout. I just can't get you out of my

head. Boy, it's more than I dare to think a - bout. I just

think a - bout. Ev - 'ry night, e - ve - ry day.

(Bridge 2 see block lyrics)

Just to___ be there___ in___ your___ arms.___ Won't you___

Bridge 2:
There's a dark secret in me
Don't leave me locked in your heart
Set me free
Feel the need in me.

Beautiful

Words & Music by Linda Perry

© Copyright 2002 Stuck In The Throat/Famous Music LLC, USA.
All Rights Reserved. International Copyright Secured.

2. E♭   E♭7/D♭

- day.   No mat-ter what_ we do,_____ no mat-ter what_ we say,_

Cm   B

___ we're the song in-side_ the tune,_____ full of beau-ti-ful mis-takes._

E♭   E♭7/D♭

And ev-'ry-where_ we go,_____ the sun will al-ways shine,_

Cm   B   **D.S. al Coda**

___ but to-mor-row we might a-wake,___ on___ the oth-er side._

⊕ Coda

E♭   E♭7/D♭   Cm   B   E♭

- day.   *Vocal ad lib.*   Don't you bring me down___ to-day.

Free time

E♭7/D♭   Cm   Bmaj7♭5   E♭

Vocal ad lib.   Don't you bring me down   to-day.___

Verse 2:
To all your friends you're delirious
So consumed in all your doom
Trying hard to fill the emptiness
The pieces gone, left the puzzle undone
Is that the way it is?

Mad World

Words & Music by Roland Orzabal

© Copyright 1982 Roland Orzabal Limited.
Chrysalis Music Limited.
All Rights Reserved. International Copyright Secured.

1. All a-round me are fa-mi-liar fa - ces, worn-out pla-ces,

(Verse 2 see block lyrics)

worn-out fa - ces. Bright and ear-ly for their dai-ly ra-ces,

go-ing no-where, go-ing no-where. Their tears are fill-ing

up their glass-es, no ex-pres-sion, no ex-pres-sion.

Hide my head, I wan-na drown my sor-row, no to-mor-row,

no to-mor-row. And I find it kin-da fun-ny, I find it kin-da

234

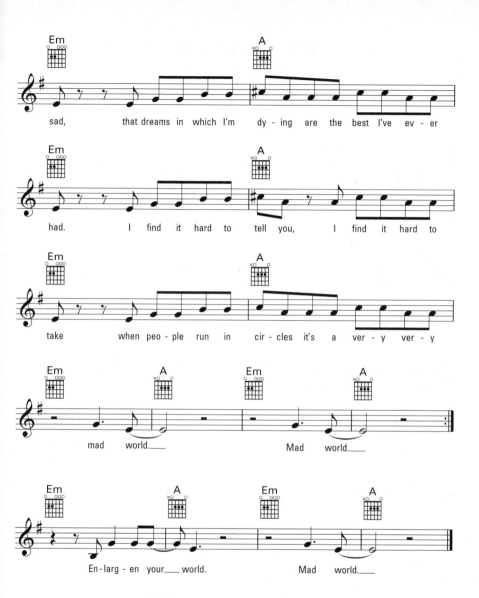

Verse 2:
Children waiting for the day they feel good
Happy Birthday, Happy Birthday
And I feel the way that every child should sit and listen, sit and listen
Went to school and I was very nervous
No one knew me, no one knew me
Hello teacher, tell me what's my lesson
Look right through me, look right through me.

Dry Your Eyes

Words & Music by Mike Skinner

© Copyright 2004 Pure Groove Music Limited.
Universal Music Publishing Limited.
All rights in Germany administered by Universal Music Publ. GmbH.
All Rights Reserved. International Copyright Secured.

Chorus

Dry your eyes mate, I know it's hard to take_ but her_mind has_ been made_ _ up. There's_ plen-ty__ more fish_ in the sea.

Dry your eyes_ mate, I know you want to make_ her see_ how much_ this pain_ _ hurts. But you've got to walk__ a-way now. It's ov - er._

To Coda
repeat twice for verses 2 & 3

And I'm just standing there, I can't say a word 'cause everything's just gone. I've got nothing, absolutely nothing.

D.S. al Coda

236

237

Verse 1:

In one single moment your whole life can turn 'round
I stand there for a minute staring straight into the ground
Looking to the left slightly then looking back down
World feels like it's caved in, proper sorry frown
Please let me show you where we could only just be for us
I can change and I can grow or we could adjust
The wicked thing about us is we always have trust
We can even have an open relationship if you must
I look at her, she stares almost straight back at me
But her eyes glaze over like she's looking straight through me
Then her eyes must have closed for what seems an eternity
When they open up she's looking down at her feet.
(Chorus)

Verse 2:

So then I moved my hand up from down by my side
Shaking, my life was crashing before my eyes
Turned the palm of my hand up to face the skies
Touched the bottom of her chin and let out a sigh
'Cause I can't imagine my life without you and me
There's things I can't imagine doing, things I can't imagine seeing
It weren't supposed to be easy surely?
Please, please I'm begging, please
She brings her hands up towards where my hands are rested
She wraps her fingers 'round mine with the softness she's blessed with
She peels away my fingers, looks at me and then gestures
By pushing my hand away to my chest from hers.
(Chorus)

Verse 3:

Trying to pull her close out of bare desperation
Put my arms around her, trying to change what she's saying
Pull my head level with hers so she might engage in
Look into her eyes to make her listen again
I'm not gonna fuckin', just fuckin' leave it all now
'Cause you said it would be forever and that was your vow
And you're gonna let our thing simply crash and fall down
You're well out of order now, this is well out of town
She pulls away, my arms are tightly clamped around her waist
Gently pushes me back as she looks at me straight
Turns around so she's now got her back to my face
Takes one step forward, looks back, and then walks away.
(Chorus)

Grace Kelly

Words & Music by Jodi Marr, Dan Warner, John Merchant & Michael Penniman

© Copyright 2005 Universal Music Publishing Limited (80%) (administered in Germany by Universal Music Publ. GmbH)/
Sony/ATV Music Publishing (UK) Limited (10%)/
Famous Music Publishing Limited (10%).
All Rights Reserved. International Copyright Secured.

"I wanna talk to you". "The last time we talked Mr Smith, 1. Do I at-tract you, do I re-
you reduced me to tears. I promise you it won't happen again."

- pulse you with my quea-sy smile?___ Am I too dir-ty, am I too flir-ty, do I like what you like?_

___ I could be whole-some, I could be loath-some, guess I'm a lit-tle bit___ shy._

___ Why don't you like me, why don't you like me with-out mak-ing me try?_

___ I try to be like Grace Kel-ly___ but all her looks were too sad._

___ So I try a lit-tle Fred-die._ I've gone i-den-ti-ty

mad. I could be brown, I could be blue, I could be vi-o-let

sky. I could be hurt-ful, I could be pur-ple, I could be a-ny-thing you like.

Got-ta be green, got-ta be mean, got-ta be ev-'ry-thing more. Why don't you like me? Why don't you

To Coda II

like me? Why don't you walk out_ the door?___ (Getting angry doesn't solve anything.)

To Coda I

2. How can I help it, how can I help it, how can I help what you think? Hel-lo my ba-by, hel-lo my

ba-by, put-ting my life on the brink. Why don't you like me, why don't you like me, why don't you like_ your-

D.S. al Coda I

-self? Should I bend ov-er, should I look old-er just to be put on your shelf?

Coda I

Say what you want to sat - is-fy_ your-self.__

But you on-ly want what ev - 'ry-bo - dy else_ says you_ should want._____ You want._____

D.S.S. al Coda II

Coda II

like me? Walk out the door.___ I could be brown, I could be blue, I could be vi - o - let sky. I could be hurt-ful, I could be pur-ple, I could be a-ny-thing you like. Got-ta be green, got-ta be mean, got-ta be ev-'ry-thing more. Why don't you like me? Why don't you like me? Walk out the door.__

Ooh._____ (Humphrey, we're leaving.)

241

Hung Up

Words & Music by Benny Andersson, Bjorn Ulvaeus, Madonna & Stuart Price

© Copyright 2005 Union Songs AB, Sweden/Bocu Music Limited (50%)/
Warner/Chappell Music Limited (50%).
All rights in Germany administered by Universal Music Publ. GmbH.
All Rights Reserved. International Copyright Secured.

242

243

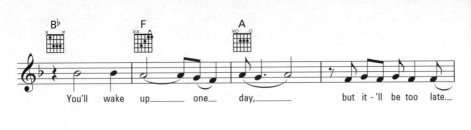

You'll wake up___ one___ day,___ but it-'ll be too late.___

Ev-'ry lit-tle thing that you say or do,___ I'm hung up, I'm hung___

up on you.___ Wait-ing for your call, ba-by, night and day,___ I'm fed up,

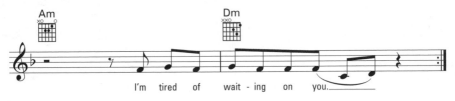

I'm tired of wait-ing on you.___

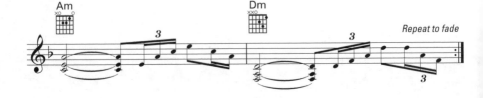

Repeat to fade

244

America

Words & Music by Johnny Borrell & Andy Burrows

© Copyright 2006 Sony/ATV Music Publishing (UK) Limited.
All Rights Reserved. International Copyright Secured.

Oh, oh, oh,____ oh! There's trou - ble in A - me - ri - ca.

Oh, oh, oh,_____ oh._____

2. Yes - ter - day was ea - sy, hap - pi - ness came and went.__
(Verse 3 see block lyrics)

I got the mo - vie script,__ but I don't know what__ it meant.__

I light a ci - gar - ette__'cause I can't get__ no____ sleep. There's

no - thing on the TV, no - thing on the ra - di - o that means that much__ to me.__ There's

no - thing on the TV, no - thing on the ra - di - o that I can be - lieve____ in.

All my life,— I'm watch-ing A-me-ri-ca.

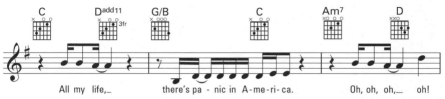

All my life,— there's pa-nic in A-me-ri-ca. Oh, oh, oh,— oh!

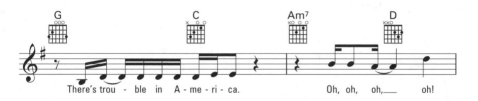

There's trou-ble in A-me-ri-ca. Oh, oh, oh,— oh!

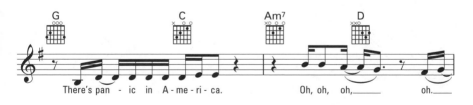

There's pan-ic in A-me-ri-ca. Oh, oh, oh,— oh.—

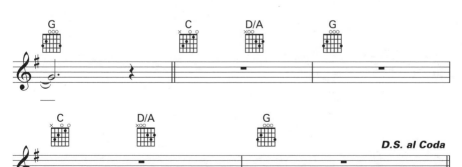

D.S. al Coda

✛ Coda

C   D   G/B   C^{add9}

_ stand me up, don't let me down,_ no,   I need you_ to-night,_   to hold_

C   D   G/B   C^{add9}

_____ me.   Say you'll_ be here,   and

C   D   G/B   C^{add9}   C   D

hold_____ me.   Say you'll_ be here,   and hold_____ me.

G/B   C^{add9}   C   D   G/B   C^{add9}

Say you'll_ be here,   and hold._____

Am⁷   D   G   C

All my life___   I'm watch-ing A-me-ri-ca.

Am⁷   D   G   C

All my life___   there's pa - nic in A-me-ri-ca.

Am⁷   D   G   C

Oh, oh, oh,___ oh!   She's lost___ in A-me-ri-ca.

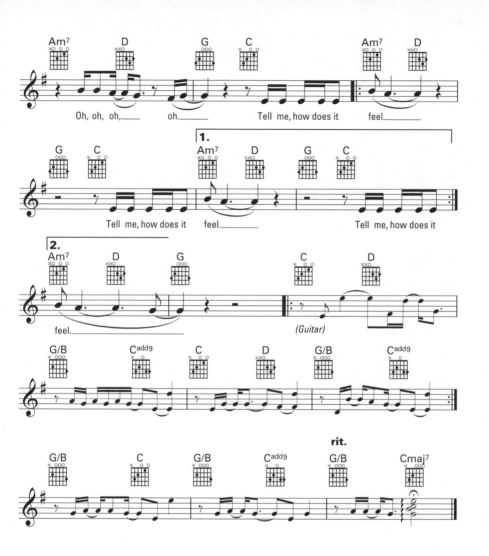

Verse 3:
Yesterday was easy
Yes, I got the news
When you get it straight you stand up
You just can't lose
Give you my confidence
All my faith in life
Don't stand me up, don't let me down
No, I need you tonight, to hold me...

Crazy

Words & Music by Thomas Callaway, Brian Burton, Gianfranco Reverberi & Gian Piero Reverberi

© Copyright 2006 Chrysalis Music Limited (35%)/
Warner/Chappell Music Publishing (35%)/
Atmosphere Music Limited (30%).
All Rights Reserved. International Copyright Secured.

1. I re-mem-ber when, I re-mem-ber, I re-mem-ber when I lost my mind.

There was some-thing so plea-sant a-bout_ that place.

Ev-en your e-mo-tions had an e-cho in so much space.

2. And when you're out there, with-out care, yeah, I was out of touch.
(Verse 3 see block lyrics)

But it was-n't be-cause_ I did-n't know e-nough.

I just knew too much.

G   Cm

Does that make me cra - zy?____   Does that make me cra-

(3° see block lyrics)

E♭maj⁷   A♭add9

- zy?____   Does that make me cra - zy?____

A♭   Gsus⁴

Pos - sib - ly._____

G   C

To Coda ⊕

And I hope that you__ are hav-

A♭add9   A♭

- ing__ the time of__your life.____   But think twice,__

E♭maj⁷   Gsus⁴   G

that's my on - ly ad - vice.__

Cm

4. Ev - er since I was lit - tle, ev - er since I was lit - tle it looked like fun.__

And it's no co-in - ci - dence_ I've come_____

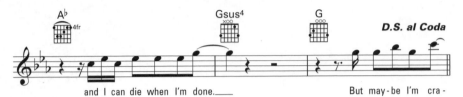

and I can die when I'm done.____

D.S. al Coda

But may-be I'm cra-

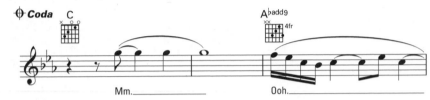

Coda

Mm._____ Ooh._____

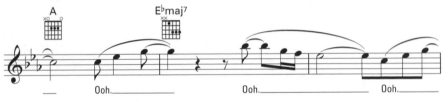

Ooh._____ Ooh._____ Ooh.

_____ Ooh._____ Ooh.__ Mm._____

Verse 3:
Come on now, who do you
Who do you, who do you
Who do you think you are?
Ha, ha, ha, bless your soul
You really think you're in control
Well, I think you're crazy
I think you're crazy
I think you're crazy just like me.

My heroes had the heart
To lose their lives out on a limb
And all I remember is thinking
I wanna be like them.

On 𝄋:
But maybe I'm crazy
Maybe you're crazy
Maybe we're crazy
Probably.

Smile

Words & Music by Jackie Mittoo, Clement Dodd, Iyiola Babalola, Darren Lewis & Lily Allen

© Copyright 2006 Universal Music Publishing Limited (50%)/
Sparta Florida Music Group Limited (50%).
All rights in Germany administered by Universal Music Publ. GmbH.
All Rights Reserved. International Copyright Secured.

♩ = 96

1. When you first left me, I was wanting
(Verse 2 see block lyrics)
more, but you were do-ing that girl next door, what'd you do that
for? When you first left me, I did-n't know what to
say. I'd nev-er been on my own that way, just sat by my-
-self all day. I was so lost back then,
but, with a lit-tle help_ from my friends, I found the light in the tun-nel at the end._

F   Gm

Now you're call - ing me up on the phone,

F

so you can have a lit - tle whine and a moan,

Gm   F

it's on - ly be-cause you're feel - ing a - lone.

Gm⁷   Fmaj⁷

At first, when I see you cry, it makes me

Gm⁷   Fmaj⁷

smile, yeah, it makes me smile.

Gm⁷   Fmaj⁷

At worst, I feel bad for a while, but then I just

1.

Gm⁷   Fmaj⁷

smile, I go a - head and smile. 2. When -

Verse 2:
Whenever you see me, you say that you want me back
And I tell you it don't mean jack, no it don't mean jack
I couldn't stop laughing, no, no I just couldn't help myself
See, you messed up my mental health, I was quite unwell.

Bleeding Love

Words & Music by Ryan Tedder & Jesse McCartney

© Copyright 2007 Write 2 Live Publishing/Jambition Music, USA.
Kobalt Music Publishing Limited (66.67%)/
Warner/Chappell Artemis Music Limited (33.33%).
All Rights Reserved. International Copyright Secured.

But I don't care what they say, I'm in love with you. They try to pull me a-way,

but they don't know the truth. My heart's crip-pled by the vein that I keep on clos-

-ing. You cut me o-pen and I keep bleed-ing, keep

keep bleed-ing love. I keep bleed-ing, I keep keep bleed-ing love.

Keep bleed-ing, keep keep bleed-ing love.

To Coda

You cut me o-pen, ooh.

Try-ing hard not to hear but they talk so loud,

their pierc-ing sounds fill my ears, try to fill me with doubt, yet I know that the

goal is to keep me from fall - ing,___ hey, yeah.___

But noth-ing's great-er than the rush that comes with your em- brace, and in this world of lone-

- li-ness I see your face,___ yet ev-'ry-one a-round___ me thinks that I'm go ing cra-

- zy.___ May - be, may - be.

D.S. al Coda

Coda

And it's drain - ing all___ of me.___ Oh, they

find it hard___ to be - lieve,___ I'll be wear-ing these scars___ for ev-

258

Umbrella

Words & Music by Christopher Stewart, Terius Nash, Shawn Carter & Thaddis Harrell

© Copyright 2007 Warner/Chappell Music Limited (40%)/
Peermusic (UK) Limited (40%)/
EMI Music Publishing Limited (10%)/
Sony/ATV Music Publishing (UK) Limited (10%).
All Rights Reserved. International Copyright Secured.

♩ = 85

N.C.

Spoken: Uh-huh uh-huh, yeah, Rihanna. Uh-huh uh-huh, good

girl gone bad. Uh-huh uh-huh, take three... action. Uh-huh uh-huh, no

Eh eh eh,
clouds in my storms, let it rain, I hydroplane into fame, comin' down with the Dow Jones. When the

eh eh eh eh.
clouds come we gone, we Rocafella, she fly higher than weather and she rocks it better.

You know me an anticipation for precipitation, stacks chips for the rainy day

Eh eh eh, eh eh eh eh. 1. You
Jay rain man is back with little Ms. Sunshine Rihanna, where you at?

262

Verse 2:
These fancy things, will never come inbetween
You're part of my entity, here for infinity
When the world has took its part
When the world has dealt its cards
If the hand is hard, together we'll mend your heart.

263

Hallelujah

Words & Music by Leonard Cohen

© Copyright 1984 Sony/ATV Music Publishing (UK) Limited.
All Rights Reserved. International Copyright Secured.

lu..._____ Hal - le - lu - jah. Hal - le -

- lu - jah.__ Hal - le - lu - jah. Hal - le - lu - jah.__

Verse 2:
Well, your faith was strong but you needed proof
You saw her bathing on the roof
Her beauty and the moonlight overthrew ya
And she tied you to her kitchen chair
And she broke your throne and she cut your hair
And from your lips she drew the Hallelujah.

Verse 3:
Well, baby, I've been here before
I've seen this room, and I've walked this floor
You know, I used to live alone before I knew you
And I've seen your flag on the marble arch
And love is not a victory march
It's a cold and it's a broken Hallelujah.

Verse 4:
Well, there was a time when you let me know
What's really going on below
But now you never show that to me, do ya?
But remember when I moved in you
And the holy dove was moving too
And every breath we drew was Hallelujah?

Verse 5:
Maybe there's a God above
But all I've ever learned from love
Was how to shoot somebody who outdrew ya
And it's not a cry that you hear at night
It's not somebody who's seen the light
It's a cold and it's a broken Hallelujah.

Viva La Vida

Words & Music by Guy Berryman, Chris Martin, Jon Buckland & Will Champion

© Copyright 2008 Universal Music Publishing MGB Limited.
All rights in Germany administered by Musik Edition Discoton GmbH (a division of Universal Music Publishing Group).
All Rights Reserved. International Copyright Secured.

(Verse 3 see block lyrics)

266

Lis-tened as the crowd_____ would sing,_____ "Now the old king is dead,_ long live the king." One min-ute I held the key,_ _ next the walls were closed on me and I dis-cov-ered that my cas - tles stand_____ up - on pil-lars of salt_ and pil-lars of sand. I hear Je - ru - sa-lem bells_____ a - ring - ing. Ro - man Cav-al - ry choirs_____ are sing - ing. Be my mir-ror, my sword,_

Verse 2:
It was the wicked and wild wind
Blew down the doors to let me in
Shattered windows and the sound of drums
People couldn't believe what I'd become
Revolutionaries wait for my head on a silver plate
Just a puppet on a lonely string
Oh, who would ever wanna be king?

Mercy

Words & Music by Duffy & Stephen Booker

© Copyright 2007 EMI Music Publishing Limited (60%)/
Universal Music Publishing Limited (40%) (administered in Germany by Universal Music Publ. GmbH).
All Rights Reserved. International Copyright Secured.

I'm un - der your spell._____ You got me beg-ging you for mer- cy.

Why won't you re-lease_____ me? You got me beg-ging you for mer - cy.

Why won't you re-lease___me? I said_ re-lease_____ me.

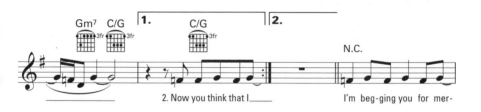

_____ 2. Now you think that I_____ I'm beg-ging you for mer-

- cy, just__ why won't____you re-lease___me? I'm beg-ging you for mer -

- cy. You got me beg-ging, You got me beg- ging, You got me beg- ging.

Verse 2:
Now you think that I will be something on the side
But you got to understand that I need a man
Who can take my hand
Yes I do!

272

2 3 4 5 6 7 8 9